IF I LIVE TO BE 100

Crown Publishers

New York

IF I LIVE TO BE 100

Lessons from the Centenarians

NEENAH ELLIS

Grateful acknowledgment is made to Graywolf Press for permission to reprint an excerpt from "Otherwise" from *Otherwise: New & Selected Poems* by Jane Kenyon, copyright © 1996 by the Estate of Jane Kenyon. Reprinted by permission of Graywolf Press, Saint Paul, Minnesota.

Published by Crown Publishers, New York, New York.
Member of the Crown Publishing Group, a division of Random House, Inc.
www.randomhouse.com

CROWN is a trademark and the Crown colophon is a registered trademark of Random House, Inc.

Printed in the United States of America

DESIGN BY BARBARA STURMAN

Library of Congress Cataloging-in-Publication Data
Ellis, Neenah.
If I live to be 100 : lessons from the centenarians / by Neenah Ellis.
1. Centenarians—United States—Interviews. I. Title.
HQ1060.5 .E45   2002
305.26′092′273—dc21   2002024709

ISBN 0-609-60842-8

10 9 8 7 6 5 4 3 2

To wonderful parents,
Bee and Jen Ellis

CONTENTS

Introduction   3

1   VICTORIA WILLIAMS   11
          "You people have so much fun now."

2   ELLA MILLER   23
          "Everybody drank water . . . and it was good."

3   MONA BRECKNER   31
               "I tried to do my part."

4   ANNA WILMOT   47
          "I tell you, I'm something, aren't I?"

5   ABRAHAM GOLDSTEIN   63
              *"You don't live in the past,
               you live in the present."*

6   MARGARET RAWSON   79
          *"We used to go out into the park in back
                   and eat lunch."*

CONTENTS

7   **HARRY SHAPIRO**   89

"Shapiro was here."

8   **SADIE AND GILBERT HILL**   101

"Sadie can't sleep past six o'clock."

9   **RUTH ELLIS I**   113

"I'm just an ordinary person."

10   **LOUISIANA HINES I**   129

"You know, people used to sell people a long time ago."

11   **RUTH ELLIS II**   137

"They just want to know me 'cause I'm a hundred."

12   **ROY LARKIN STAMPER I**   145

"I need a companion, real bad."

13   **HELEN BOARDMAN**   165

"I guess I'm an optimist."

14   **THOMAS LEWIS**   181

"The thing that will make you happy, nobody tells you."

CONTENTS

15   MARION COWEN   193
"I just accept my life day by day."

16   RUTH ELLIS III   207
"I just want to get out of this world."

17   ROY LARKIN STAMPER II   215
"If we live together six months or a day,
at least we're together."

18   LOUISIANA HINES II   223
"It means something to do good. It does.
It means something."

19   HARRY BOEFF   233
"Gee, I'm really telling you everything,
aren't I?"

Afterword   249

Acknowledgments   255

IF I LIVE TO BE 100

INTRODUCTION

I OPEN MY EYES to daylight in the tent. Six-thirty. Surely Anna can't be up yet. I peer out through the pines toward the glassy lake to look for her.

It's the morning after Anna's birthday and my tent is pitched a few feet from her bedroom window. She liked the idea of my camping here; it appealed to her sense of adventure. She is fun-loving but not foolish. When I asked her last night, she thought for a second before answering.

"Yes, okay. That would be okay."

It had been a long day. I'd arrived at her home in western Massachusetts at noon and her cabin was already noisy with visitors; the phone was ringing, and Anna and her son, Freddie, were greeting everyone boisterously.

"Hey, you made it!" She held open the screen door for me. I gave her my present right away.

"Wow! You didn't have to do that!" I'd brought a bottle of champagne.

"Should we open it now?" Anna said. "No, wait, I'm gonna save it for later. Come on in and make yourself at home."

She brought me into the living room, bright with August light but cool on this breezy point.

"Come and see what I got," she said, heading for the screened porch. On a table in the corner was a vase of long-stemmed red roses. The blooms reached higher than Anna and four feet across.

"Guess how many?" she asked, as if I didn't know. "A hundred and three." She leaned toward me for emphasis. "One for each year." Her smile seemed to know things I couldn't imagine.

Anna Wilmot was born in 1898.

MORE PEOPLE arrived and she hurried to greet them. Neighbors and relatives and longtime friends had brought their children, and birthday cards and gifts. Some had taken off work to be here. A six-year-old girl gave Anna a bucket full of presents: pencils, stickers, a seashell, a hand-colored page torn out of a coloring book, and a card she'd made herself. A young woman who was leaving soon for college said she just *had* to stop by. Anna knew all their stories; she asked about their families, catching up on their news. She hugged everyone, read their cards aloud, and passed them around the room for others to admire.

"That's a real hot one!" she said now and then.

In a while Anna and all her guests left to walk to a neighbor's house down the road. Anna leaned on her old broken shovel handle to support herself as she limped along. More people were waiting to wish her a happy birthday on the neighbor's patio by the lake.

We stayed all afternoon. There was wine and soft drinks and hot dogs and salads and, finally, a chocolate sheet cake that said: KEEP ON ROWING.

We went back to Anna's afterward and retold stories

we'd heard, and at 8:45, Anna announced, "I'm dead!" and went to bed.

IT'S EIGHT O'CLOCK the next morning. I throw off the sleeping bag and reach for the tent zipper. As I sweep the hair off my face, I see her green rowboat on the lake; she's pulling on the oars, moving steadily across the silvery water, heading back to her launching beach. She's already coming in. I rush down through the trees to the water and she glides toward me.

"Hey, you're up already!" she says.

I had not asked to go along with Anna this morning. She had taken me out for a boat ride when I stopped by a couple of weeks earlier, but she wouldn't take me early in the morning. "It will be too cold for you," she said. (It was August 1.) Anna protects her time alone, so she went out in the morning and again at midday with me. I carried the oars down the footpath from her house and she followed, holding on to a wooden railing. She has arthritis in her knees and she grunted with each step down.

"You've got to push yourself, you know?" she said.

There's a name painted in black on the side of the flat-bottomed boat: GRANNIE ANNIE. It was half out of the water and tied to a tree. She directed me to sit in the stern. Then she laid the oars in and, steadying herself on the gunwales, slowly lifted first one foot, then the other, into the boat. I helped put the oars into the oarlocks as she got seated. Anna grabbed the oar handles and then pushed on them hard, but the boat was touching bottom. We both jerked our bodies away from the shore and it floated free. She rowed confidently and slowly, with small strokes, bringing the boat out around the point and into the center of the lake. We sat knee-to-knee. I felt happy but useless. She gave me the role of navigator.

"Am I headed for the island?"

"Directly," I said.

"Can you see the bottom? It's pretty shallow here."

I could.

"You know, you could go in if you want. Take off your clothes and go right in. Go ahead. Why not?" Anna laughed but she meant it. I know she's done it herself.

I'VE ALWAYS thought I would live to one hundred. When I was eight years old, a girl who lived down the road from us in rural Indiana showed me the lifeline on my palm and told me that a long line meant a long life. I believed her because she was two years older than I was and owned Beatles records. I stood in her backyard by the swing and traced the crease all the way around to the top of my hand.

And around that same time, at the Newton Yost Elementary School Fair, a gypsy confirmed my findings. When I found out that the gypsy was really my brother's fourth-grade teacher, Mrs. Renfro, in hoop earrings, and not a real gypsy, I was not dissuaded. She was a real *teacher* and they don't lie.

As an adult, I have new reasons to believe. My grandmother is ninety-nine. Since I was a child she's been telling us that she wouldn't live much longer, but now she's on her second pacemaker. Never mind that she's blind in one eye and often forgets which pills she's taken. She's decided she's "gonna make it." But I only recently started thinking about what my life might be like at one hundred.

In 1997 I got a grant from the Corporation for Public Broadcasting to do a radio series, an oral history of the twentieth century. I'd proposed that I would interview hundred-year-old people—centenarians—and ask them about the past. Some told such vivid stories that I felt transported in time. Some wanted to talk about their work, some about their children, others about their parents or spouses, now long dead, or their God, who was very much alive. I sat with them for hours and sometimes days at a time. Our conversations became the basis for a radio series on National Public Radio's *Morning Edition* in 2000 called "One Hundred Years of Stories."

But after a while, as much as I love history, I wanted to know about their lives in the present tense. Most of the centenarians were models of perseverance and positive thinking. They had open minds and open hearts. They were curious and generous and fun.

I had stumbled upon a demographic group that I had not known existed: hundred-year-old people who, unlike most people their age, suffer no dementia, have never had a major illness, and remain engaged with the world.

As I listened to their life stories, I realized that I was being given the chance to choose my own future, like Ebenezer Scrooge. By lining my life up alongside theirs, I got a better idea of where I might be headed. I'd always had a sense of my life as a leaf floating down a river, on a course that seemed unalterable, but suddenly, in my mid-forties, I felt the need to make more choices: I could decide what sort of old person I wanted to be.

Where will I live? What work will I do? Will I be lonely? Will I be a good companion to my older husband? Will I always be without children? How can I be a better sister to my siblings at a distance? A friend to friends as we all endure loss? How will I keep nature in my life? How will I stay healthy?

And so, instead of asking only about the past, I tried to learn what made the centenarians' lives worth living for so long.

In my early conversations with them, I was too focused on their physical problems. I was too often in a hurry, looking for facts instead of truth. I was embarrassed to ask about sex, afraid to ask about death, and assumed I could not come right out with "What is the meaning of life?" And I was uncomfortable with silence.

But I got better. And as I tried to put what I learned from the centenarians into those monthly nine-minute radio stories, I realized I wouldn't get my answers by asking questions, I would get them by waiting.

In her essay "Tell Me More: On the Fine Art of Listening," Brenda Ueland describes the rewards of being a patient listener:

> Suddenly you begin to hear not only what people are saying, but what they are trying to say, and you sense the whole truth about them. And you sense existence, not piecemeal, not this object and that, but as a translucent whole.

The centenarians are as mysterious as infants in their way—so full of promise and surprises—even if they are sometimes confused. They use funny, archaic expressions, they have strong regional accents, and their old bodies have a different language, too. I love to see how they are dressed, what they eat, what they think is funny.

I feel comfortable with them physically. I like it when they want to hold my hand and sit close because they can't hear or see. I like the cool, slippery skin on their hands and the way their eyes light up. I love to see a hundred-year-old woman wearing lipstick.

There is a glow, a magnetism, a vibe I feel when I'm around them. It causes me to feel a deep connection and I learned a scientific explanation for it. Some call it "limbic resonance," the innate ability of mammals to feel one another's emotional state. It's a primal source of human happiness. Learning about it helped me slow down and be comfortable with silence, to welcome it.

This is my story about learning to listen.

1

VICTORIA WILLIAMS

"You people have so much fun now."

VICTORIA WILLIAMS, at 106 years old, was the size of a twelve-year-old girl. They brought her to me in a wheelchair. On the seat next to her was a black vinyl pocketbook, its stiff handle placed up over her shoulder. Her lips were pressed tight together. She was angry.

The health aide pushing the chair rolled her eyes as she approached me in the visitors lounge and said in a low voice, "We've had a rough morning."

"Miss Williams, would you like a cookie?" she said, coming around to the front of the chair.

"I want coffee," said Victoria Williams, loudly. The woman walked off without introducing us.

"Good morning," I said in my most chipper voice. Victoria Williams stared at me like a bug, expressionless. I leaned toward her. There was a faint smell of urine.

"I'm the reporter who's come to interview you."

"Interview me?"

"For radio. I just want to ask you some questions about your life."

VICTORIA WILLIAMS was the first centenarian I met. I had applied for a grant from the Corporation for Public Broadcasting to interview centenarians and I needed a sample tape, to give the review panel an idea of what my radio series might sound like. I was in a hurry; the deadline was soon.

I called the Washington Center for Aging Services, a huge home for the elderly in Northeast D.C. It's not the kind of place I would choose to live in. The aides seemed caring but stretched hopelessly beyond their means. I was taken to a lounge area where residents sat silently, some watching television, some in a stupor.

I was not surprised to find myself there for the first interview. It matched my stereotypes and I thought, This is what happens when you're old if you have no place else to go. I expected to see many more places like this. I also expected, at that time, that most centenarians would be like Victoria Williams.

The skin on her face was smooth and shiny and taut. She jutted her jaw, sliding her false teeth forward and then back, inspecting me, shifting her attention away from her struggle with the aide, whatever it had been.

"Here's your coffee, Miss Williams." The aide returned with a steaming Styrofoam cup and two chocolate-chip cookies on a napkin. Evidently, it was a peace offering, and it was accepted.

With her elbows on the armrests and her dark, bony fingers wrapped delicately around the cup, Victoria Williams held the coffee beneath her nose, inhaling the vapor.

"My mother and father died and we had to go to work," she started in abruptly, without looking up.

"You went to work after they passed on?"

"Part-time? No! We didn't no *part-time,* we worked if it was all day or all night."

I shifted closer to her right ear so she could hear me better.

She sipped the coffee loudly and said, "Ooh, that's hot!" Then she continued: "We had to work all the time. Didn't no place stay and pay no rent. No! We worked! We stay where we worked."

She put the edge of the cookie between her teeth and broke off a piece, chewing as she talked, not looking at me.

"You people have so much *fun* now."

I wasn't sure whom she meant.

"You think people have more fun now?"

"Yeah, you all have a *lot* of fun, setting down and drinking coffee that somebody make and give you. You didn't make and give *us* none. We had to make our own."

"Miss Williams, do you remember when you were a little girl?"

"A little girl."

"Do you remember?"

"When?"

"When you were a girl. Do you remember?"

"Yeaaaahh." She dragged out the word and smiled.

"What was it like when you were a little girl?"

"We used to know a *lot* of little girls in our day," she said.

"No, I mean when *you* were a little girl."

"I was in school. There were a lot of little girls."

"Where did you go to school?"

"Wherever Mother worked, if it wasn't too far for us to walk, we'd go in that school."

"You walked to school?"

"Yeah. The teachers were nice to us, too. There weren't no nasty teachers."

"What did you learn in school, what did you study?"

"Studied everything. Graduated. Mmm-hmm. Teachers were nice to us."

Before long it became clear that Victoria Williams could tell only one story about herself and she kept coming back to it, as if it were a tape playing in her mind: She graduated from high school and then from Hampton Institute in Virginia, one of the country's first black universities, and then she taught school. She got work because she was highly recommended. People respected her parents, who were honest and hardworking, so she had "good backing" and got good jobs. She kept coming back to parts of this story no matter what question I asked. Often she would break into a remembered conversation, speaking both parts.

I asked her, "Where was your daddy from?"

"My daddy's son?"

"No, where was he *from*?"

"When did he . . . ?"

"Where was he born?"

"Where? I forgot. My daddy was born somewhere in New York or New Jersey. My mother was a teacher. She cooked and washed and ironed and taught school, too, so she had a good recommendation."

"Do you know where your mother was born?"

"Yeah! She was born down in North Carolina."

"And where were you born?"

"North Carolina."

"What town?"

"Near Hampton Institute. That was the hospital where people used to go in. People didn't have their babies out in the street. You'd have your baby in the hospital with a doctor, and when the baby's born, the doctor would say, 'She was a healthy child,' and they'd take you right in school. So the background helps to push you. Yeah. And then you get you another teacher and you do pretty good. 'Well, where did you learn that?' 'I learned that at such and such a school.' 'Oh, you went to more than one school?' 'Yes I did!' "

After an hour or so, I began to feel frustrated, deciding that I couldn't have a real exchange of ideas with Victoria Williams. There would be no stories from the early part of the century, only fragments of memories that I had no hope of putting in context. I'd just try to get some good one-liners and leave. Luckily, though, the health aide was listening in and had more patience than I.

"When you were coming up, when you were a little girl, did you hear much about slavery?" she asked Miss Williams.

"We didn't know much about slavery. We learned about the college part of a colored person. No indeed, we were above that! Yes. Mmm-hmm. He has to either be in college or have finished. He can't be out in the street. You can't teach him nothin' in the street. You can help him after he got in college."

In my deaf impatience, I failed to realize the richness of this question and changed the subject.

"Miss Williams, do you remember when you came to Washington?"

AFTER A COUPLE of hours, I said good-bye. The interview had mostly been a failure. I had no coherent stories and only a vague idea of what her life had been like.

A couple of days later I interviewed another lady; this one had only just turned one hundred.

"Rochelle" had a small, sunny apartment in an assisted-living facility. She was high-spirited and bossy but sweet, too, and a little loopy the day I met her. She assumed she knew what questions I had and insisted on telling me right away why she had lived so long.

"Ever since I was a kid, I drew people like flies and I still do. When I come down to dinner—I'm not showing off, I'm telling you the truth—there's a lineup that passes me. Honest to God, I'm not lying to you. People admire the hundred age, but people have *always* been drawn to me. That's one thing I can really boast about. I always had friends."

She seemed nervous and impatient, and wanted to get this over with. I raced through a list of questions I had prepared in an effort to do a better interview than I had with Victoria Williams. The questions involved most of the major historical events of the twentieth century. But Rochelle had a fuzzy memory for some things. She couldn't remember the difference between World War I and World War II.

"Oh, now I'm confused," she said, her hands fluttering above her lap, but with some prompting, she did recall the end of World War I. She was living in New York at the time.

"I remember the excitement. People went out in the street, they were so happy! They were so happy!"

Her eyes suddenly welled up.

"It brings tears to my eyes. *That* I remember distinctly. I was married by that time. I remember them rejoicing when the war was over."

She surprised me. One moment she seemed scattered and confused, the next moment she cried. I didn't know where to go from there.

"Tell me about your husband," I asked.

"Ahhh, that's a story in itself. There isn't much to tell. I fell in love because of his kiss. I fell in love immediately; nothing else mattered. And now, in my old age, I take inventory."

She leaned forward conspiratorily and mouthed the word "Nothing!"

She leaned back and paused. "I'd rather you wouldn't write about my husband. I thought I loved him. It was just a physical attraction. But," she said, "we were very happy. We had two beautiful children."

I could not imagine telling a stranger such a thing. I hadn't been with her more than twenty minutes. I think part of her was upset that she had revealed so much.

Rochelle said, "My mind is going. I can sense it. I don't know what happens. I become confused. I don't know what the hell I'm doing half the time."

Rochelle was aware that she was losing control and it made her agitated in conversation with a stranger. The walls of her apartment were covered with photos of her children and grandchildren and great-grandchildren, and I felt glad to know she was surrounded by people who loved her, who knew her story, who didn't care whether she could remember the difference between World War I and World War II. My presence was a reminder that she had changed and I made her uneasy.

FROM THOSE two first encounters I learned to be more patient, to spend more time. But I took those interviews and made my sample tape for the grant proposal. I chose a recording of a bittersweet Scott Joplin piano piece and played the edited tape cuts over that, with the non sequiturs edited out.

I won the grant. I promised to interview twenty centenarians around the country, but I would need a better strategy. I needed to get them to tell me stories instead of one-liners. I knew how to do this, I'd been doing it for twenty years, but never with people who had so many difficulties. The dementia, especially, was a new factor and I expected to encounter it repeatedly.

I would have to relearn what I knew about interviewing, and I would have to edit these interviews in a way that would make the centenarians sound coherent without completely misrepresenting their mental condition.

The sample tape had a pleasant enough sound to it, but I did leave in a hint of Victoria Williams's disorganized mind.

"Miss Williams, I see you have your purse with you."

"Yeah, I carry it everywhere I go. That's my driving permit and things. Because I might run into something."

"You still driving?"

"Yeah. And if someone said, 'You have a driving permit?' 'Certainly, I do.'"

"Do you still have your car?"

"Yeah. I have a car. Mmm-hmm."

"You *did* have a car."

"I *do* have a car, but I don't need it, so I leave it for my mother to drive."

2

ELLA MILLER

*"Everybody drank water . . .
and it was good."*

TWO YEARS passed. I took a full-time job with NPR and had to put the centenarian project on hold, but a friend called and said he'd heard about a woman who lived nearby and claimed to be 117 years old.

President Clinton is on the radio as I drive to see her. He's answering questions from lawyers about Monica Lewinsky and I'm riveted. Early in my career, I was a newscaster, a reporter, and then a producer for *All Things Considered* at NPR, so when big news happened, I was able to do something about it: write scripts, make calls, edit audiotape. It felt like being part of history, if in a peripheral way. I've moved on now to journalism work without daily deadlines, but the adrenaline rush still comes when the news is hot. This is one of those great news days. I'll have to add it to my list of the century's big events.

I have an appointment to interview a woman who is 117 years old, and as I turn off the car radio and walk up her sidewalk, I have the sense that I'm walking toward the past.

I'm going to meet Mrs. Ella Miller. An article in the *Washington Post* from November 1996 says she'd voted for Bill Clinton because he showed "real leadership" and that she had stayed up all night to watch the election results come in from around the country. The reporter asked her how she made up her mind whom to vote for. "God kind of deals it to me," she said.

She lives in a Virginia suburb of Washington with her niece, who runs a visiting nurses organization. Mrs. Miller has private care at home.

I'm taken up to her bedroom, where she is waiting for me, sitting in a high-backed, upholstered chair by the window. She's petite; her hair is bright white and her brown skin has deeply etched lines. She's dressed smartly, wearing earrings with her black flowered dress. She is smiling kindly as I approach and she radiates an exquisite calm.

Two years have passed since the article showed her smiling at the camera, chin in hand, and she might have slowed a little since then, but her hearing and her eyesight seem good.

She says she was born in "eighteen and eighty," the oldest girl of five children, near Rogersville, Tennessee, which she calls "the village where I lived."

"My mother raised the family. She had to work hard in order to feed the children and raise them up. She always taught them the nice things of life. We had to go to the bottom of the hill to get water to drink out of the spring. That was our water. And she taught us to be nice people. When people came in, she'd want to know if they knew what cold water was to drink and we'd run to the spring and get her a fresh little tin bucket and everybody could have a fresh drink of water. We didn't know what these cold cans were. They didn't have them in them days. Everybody drank water, mmm-hmm, and it was good, coming through the roots of the trees. And the spring was built around these trees where people had wooden benches to sit on. It was close enough to the house to have cold water without far to go."

Mrs. Miller's speech is slow and flowing, as if she's speaking remnants of an ancient ballad. When there's a pause, she inserts a gentle mmm-hmm, as if to keep the beat. After just a few minutes of looking into Mrs. Miller's eyes, I am enthralled in the presence of such an old and kind spirit.

And her use of the language is beautiful, in spite of the gaps in logic and the failing memory. I think I am hearing the way people spoke a hundred years ago. These are her exact words:

"My mother was a beautiful laundress . . . and they made starch out of flour for them to have starch to starch the clothes and pillowcases . . . and everything was beautifully washed and ironed."

"She did that at home?"

"Mmm-hmm."

"For other people?"

"For other people, all at the village, it was almost like a laundry. People brought they things for more than one family. That was her life, making a living for us. Laundry work. Beautiful laundry. Everything was starched and ironed and hung up."

Her voice is dreamy, as if she's watching scenes in her mind and describing the action.

"I read in the paper that your parents were slaves. Is that true?"

"I don't think so. No, I don't think they were slaves, as far as I can remember now. I don't remember all the things that happened then. It seems that here lately I've been more able to forget. My mind's not clear on questions way back.

They may pass through my mind, but they don't give me a conversation. I don't hear well enough to answer questions, since I'm using these eardrums. They're good, so they say, but I don't get the benefit of them as well as I planned to do."

She's referring to her hearing aids.

Mrs. Miller's clearest memories are about her childhood: how hard her mother worked, what they ate for Sunday dinner, what the house looked like—the details that a child would notice.

"We slept on the floor. We had quilts they made. We had plenty. We's warm.

"I might have Mother's quilt. Now I *do* have her clothespins. They were made of wood, they just hangs down like two hooks on them. Since I've moved to Virginia I've lost a lot of things. A lot of people would bring memory back to me if I was close, but to think of them being a distance away, I lose kind of sight of things that we did back there, because here people don't *have* all those things, people don't *use* them, and I don't get to *see* them, and I lose memory of how they were."

She knows her memory is going. There's so much she can't remember anymore.

Mrs. Miller had no formal education—"I just remember what people have told me"—though she did go to Sunday school. "They taught us about church and good religion and how to be a good girl."

Rogersville had fewer than twelve hundred people then—about a quarter of them black—and there was no public high school. She went to work as a teenager, caring for the children of a man in Knoxville who owned a shoe store. When he moved the store to Ohio, she went along and lived there for most of the rest of her life, but today she can't recall the name of the town.

Her bad memory doesn't trouble her, though. Her Bible is nearby. She listens to Christian programs on the radio and gets taped sermons from her church. She likes the Reverend Billy Graham. She shows me her cassette player. Someone has marked the Forward button with red nail polish. "We have a devotion right here in this room every morning," she says. She indicates her nurse, Fatima, who's been listening as we talk. "She sits in that chair and me in this one. My niece comes in and joins us. This is a very religious house."

"You seem happy and peaceful, Mrs. Miller," I say.

"Well, I try to love everybody. God so loved the world that He gave His son, and if He can give that up, I can give up my life to Him. I put God in control. Not a day goes by I don't sit alone and talk to Him."

"Why do you think you lived to be so old?"

"I give God the credit. If He takes me, He'll come. Whenever He wants me, I'm ready to go. Ready to go."

She pauses at length and says gently, "Well, I think that's enough for today."

She's leaning back now, her head resting on the chair back. We've talked for less than two hours. She gives a prayer before I leave and takes my hand. Her calm has given way to exhaustion, but she prays in a firm voice for me, for her niece, and for her nurse.

MY LIST OF questions about historical events of the twentieth century never came out of my bag. Her memory wasn't good enough, but it didn't seem important, anyway. She's in a timeless, peaceful place now. I don't know that place, but I can feel its effect on her.

I get back in the car and listen to Clinton droning on and on and on.

3

MONA BRECKNER

"I tried to do my part."

A SIGN NEAR the parking lot of the Minnesota Masonic Home says DEARS CROSSING.

It's a rambling, graceful, Tudor-style building on a gently rising lawn, safe under the arms of oaks. The Minnesota River Valley is just over the hill. It's like a park here, a tempting place for a picnic or a nap on this Indian summer day.

I approach the canopy-covered entrance and see Mona Breckner before she sees me. She's peering out through the glass doors, eyes wide and expectant. She rises to meet me, full up to her four feet eight inches. She's dressed for a business meeting in colors of the season: dark green skirt and short tailored jacket, cream-colored blouse with tiny autumn leaves embroidered on the cuffs and collar. Her earrings are dainty gold starbursts with pale red stones. She's wearing white hose and patent-leather sandals. And lipstick.

She steadies herself with one hand on her walker, gold watch on her wrist, a wedding band on her finger.

"Well, helloooooo!" She smiles easily. Her eyes are blue and twinkly. You'd never guess she's 102 years old.

We make small talk about the weather, of course, both of us being native Midwesterners, but she's eager to get down to business.

"I'm sure you'll want to get started as soon as possible," she says. "I've arranged for us to talk in a private office."

I was hoping to see her room, but I follow her down a hallway. She knocks on the door, to make sure no one's there, and enters.

Mona Breckner seems completely together. She knows who I am, why I have come, and what I might ask. I take her energy at face value and assume we've got all day.

"Tell me about the farm where you grew up," I begin. "Where was it? What did the countryside look like around there?"

"Well, I should give you a little background on that, because that all makes the picture a little clearer."

She clears her throat and takes a deep breath. We talk for most of the next seven hours.

"My grandfather was an original pioneer in the Northwest Territory. He came here right after the Civil War, was discharged from the army and told he could have a forty-acre area to raise wheat."

Her grandfather brought his family from eastern Wisconsin to "the wilds of Dodge Center," near Redwing, Minnesota, on the Mississippi River. For six months the family lived in the stagecoach that brought them while Mona's grandfather built a house and learned to cope with their biggest threat: prairie grass fires.

"The grass had never been touched, of course. It was the original grass, twelve foot high. There were acres and acres of this billowing, billowing, billowing tall grass. Lightning storms were quite prevalent in the area, and if the grass got on fire, it would sweep across the countryside like a racehorse and there was no way that you could control it. And it seemed to happen frequently."

So with his wife to help him, and Mona's mother, the oldest daughter, to watch the baby, husband and wife set backfires to keep the flames away from their home.

"Now, my grandfather told me this when I was a little girl, and I feel it is *definitely* correct information." Mona does not want me to think she is exaggerating.

Mona's father was an immigrant. He came to this country with his parents from the Isle of Man in the Irish Sea. At Ellis Island, he was told to go to Minnesota and have a large family. When he got there, he met and married the girl whose parents had fought the prairie fires and together they had fourteen children. Mona was the ninth.

These stories of wild prairie land are thrilling to me. I grew up in northern Indiana, near Lake Michigan, which is the transition zone between the Eastern deciduous forest and the Central tall-grass prairie. When I was a child, the prairies had long since been plowed under, but we knew the same open skies and hot summer wind that stirred the Queen Anne's lace and sent the snowy tufts of milkweed seeds floating in the air. We lay in the same dry grass by the side of gravel roads, dissected the same Monarch butterflies, and caught the same green grasshoppers that spit tobacco juice on our hands. We knew the sounds of the katydid and the bullfrog and the mysterious whippoorwill. Mona and I both loved our outdoor lives as children.

"You know, growing up on a farm in a big family was great fun. You have all kind of experiences, baby chicks and little colts. . . . You know, our dad would say, 'Our Nellie'— our little white horse—'went down in the pasture and found a little colt.' And we searched that pasture to try to find the little haven where colts came from. And we hunted and hunted and hunted and never found any, but we knew we just didn't find the right place. He kept us going with all kinds of stories! We had wonderful parents. Makes all the difference in the world. We don't have those wonderful parents in the world anymore, I'm afraid."

Mona takes pleasure in the most mundane details of her childhood. I ask specific questions, and as she opens doors in her mind, she smiles at what she sees.

"Can you describe what Christmas was like at your house?"

"Why, yes, I think I could. The older boys would go out and try to find a little blue spruce that didn't need to grow up, and we would make our own decorations—paper chains and things—and there would be tapers to burn. Once a taper fell in my sister's lap. I'll never forget that! My brother was sitting across the room and he saw the taper fall. Her lap was full of little presents, all wrapped in paper, but my brother had it put out before it started a flame."

"What kinds of presents did you get?"

"Well, I wasn't a doll person. I was a utility person. I wanted a dustpan and a broom or maybe a wagon. I remember one year I wanted a Christmas sweater. My grandmother was a knitter, so there was a lot of excitement about that."

"What color was the sweater?"

"Red! Always red or blue or gray. I remember we had angora gray wools. We all had our angora hoods."

"What kind of coats did you have?"

"Wool coats. We had sheep. They kept the wool and had

it spun into yarn. We had knit things all the time. We had long stockings that came clear up to the thigh."

"What kind of shoes did you wear?"

"We had overshoes. They were cloth and leather with buckles that came up to your knee. You were trapped in them all day and sometimes they'd get pretty wet, but they were absolutely necessary."

"Did you have a fancy dress?"

"Oh, yes, Mother always made a fancy dress for all the girls. She was an extraordinary person. I wore blues. My sister wore pinks. She burned but I tanned."

Mona allows me to wander through her childhood, asking questions. She's content to drift along with me, refreshed, I think, by the memory of being safe in the rhythms of the natural world and a large, loving family.

Mona went to college, paid her own way, and eventually went to work for the state of Minnesota as an education specialist for developmentally disabled children.

"I always said, 'They are human beings who can make a contribution if they are given enough help to do it.' And I've said, 'Dig until you can find something that child can do, see if there isn't a talent somewhere for something.' And usually, if you dig deep enough and long enough, you'll find one."

I'm enjoying the interview and I think she is, too. Her mind is keen and she rarely digresses or has to search for words. She seems content to let me direct the flow of the conversation. I ask about the Great Depression, a confluence of economic and agricultural collapse all around the country, a decade of devastation for Midwest farmers.

The Depression in Minnesota was "a horrible, horrible time," Mona says. "People were desperate. Farm after farm was lost. People couldn't pay the taxes. Morale was way, way down. You'd get up in the morning and say, 'What have we got that's ours today?' And you wondered if it was ever going to change. And if it wasn't, you couldn't exist."

The Depression killed her father, Mona says, because he lost the farm. "He just died of a deteriorating mental condition. He was a bed patient for five years. He just couldn't believe the country he'd come to had turned out this way. He just gave up."

During those years, Mona worked for the state, driving to farms around the region in a four-door Chevrolet, with a camera and a notebook, collecting official data about how people were faring. She was chosen because she was a farm girl and would understand what she was seeing.

"This was just about the time when the dust storms came, too."

The upper Midwest suffered through dust storms in the mid-thirties just like states farther south in the so-called dust bowl.

"The dust storms came in '33, I think. That was horrible. We never had that in the Middle West. I had to go into South Dakota. They had bad reports. Washington asked us if we would make an inventory, so I took my car and I went on out. Now, I had been in all kinds of weather, but I had never run into dust storms. It was an awful feeling. You could not drive in the daytime without your lights on full blast. You just couldn't see through that dust. You couldn't see lights facing you. You almost had to meet them before you knew they were coming. It was mist that was black. A black mist. And in that part of the state, the towns were far apart. When I got to South Dakota, I thought, I'll never make it back to Minnesota.

"In South Dakota they'd had a big flair, agriculturally, for turkey ranches. Instead of crops, they would raise turkeys. There would be as many as a thousand turkeys on a ranch. That takes a lot of doing, food and water and all the care for the turkeys. Well, when I got there, I was amazed at the number of turkey feathers that were on the fences. There were strings of fencing, all of them with feathers that had pulled off the turkeys as they tried to get through the fence, looking for food. It was a fence made of turkey feathers. And I saw the turkeys! There was nothing left but the long feathers on the tail and the wings. They'd go through the fences and leave all their foliage on the fence! It was the funniest sight I ever saw! I had taken my Kodak along, so I took some pictures and thought, Make up your own minds, Washington! You better get out here and see what this is about!"

Mona Breckner, the granddaughter of pioneers, learned to have a broad view of her place in the world. Her work for the state of Minnesota eventually led her to Washington, D.C., where she met with Eleanor Roosevelt about a complicated relief program designed to send a hundred farm families from Minnesota to the Matanuska Valley in Alaska. Mona was in charge of the program for the state.

She flew in an airplane for the first time to get to Washington. It was a two-day trip. She remembers that the plane flew low to the ground.

She has vivid memories of Mrs. Roosevelt.

"I was amazed. I had only seen her in pictures. I didn't

know she was such a big woman. She was large and not particularly attractive, although she was beautifully dressed. She had the appearance and the assurance of a very well-prepared person—no question that she knew her business. You had that feeling right away when you met her, that she wasn't there just for any show, she was there to get down to real hard tacks.

"She came in the room with a kind of a flourish and a swirl of her skirt. She had a long dress on, I remember; it touched the floor. She was very impressive. She had a regality about her that really made you feel you better sit up and take notice and listen. But still, I felt on a par with her. I didn't feel that she thought she was above us; she was just somebody who had charge of this and she was going to carry it out and do a good job of it. Her whole being surrounded you with a feeling of 'I'm able and I'm gonna do a good job here and I want you to do a good job, too.' And when we were finished she said, 'Now go back and see what your resources are, give the proper departments the information they need. It's not gonna cost you a cent of money.' Well, by golly, it worked. It worked out beautifully. I'll never forget those days."

MONA ANNOUNCES that lunch will be served in the dining hall momentarily, so we take a break.

She leads the way down the hall, pushing her wheeled walker fast, introducing me to friends and Masonic Home staff members, eager to show me off. She comments on how the place is managed, the programs and services they offer, and makes it clear that she is not locked in, she could leave anytime.

The dining room is pleasant. The food, served on heavy china, is ample, if bland. Mona thinks the service is poor, but I don't notice that.

She's been thinking ahead about what we might discuss after lunch, and brings some papers out of a small compartment in her walker. She is impressed that I've come from Washington, D.C., and I suddenly realize she thinks I am a political correspondent and assumes that I am interested in her thoughts on national politics.

"Here it is." She finds a sheet of paper. "This is a list of the presidents who've served the United States from Washington through Clinton, and I have found that out of forty-two candidates, I would select only ten of them as capable of being statesmen and head of a country."

"This is based on your own reading of history, your own assessment?"

"Yep. It seems to me that nine-tenths of them had no business having been there in terms of their capacity. We've had some awfully poor demonstrations of leadership in this group. When you come to statesmen, and you really say *statesmen,* then those ten really do represent men with ability."

Mona Breckner's List of Real American Statesmen

Washington	Monroe
Adams	Lincoln
Jefferson	Theodore Roosevelt
Adams	Franklin Roosevelt
Madison	Harry Truman

I think Mona is disappointed that I'm not more interested in her analysis of history, but in the time we have left, I'd rather talk about what it's like to be one hundred and two years old. I hadn't been able to ask these questions of Victoria Williams or Ella Miller. We return to our borrowed interview room.

"Mona, do you feel wiser as you get older?" I ask.

"Well, I'm not so much learning anything new, but I'm learning how to use the things that maybe I never developed before. And when I meet a situation that I don't quite know what to do with, I go through my experience and ask myself, Did I ever deal with anything like this before and was I successful? And I review in my mind the technique that I used and I think, Well, yes, this is something I've learned and can do again and again if the occasion demands it."

"And by now you have experience with a lot of things."

"Well, you have to admit that I do."

I HAVE FOUND something of myself in Mona Breckner: a pride in her career and her professional life. I realize that in our many hours together she has only once mentioned that she was married, and I know very little about her personal and emotional life.

She married late, it turns out, and had no children; her husband died after a long illness when Mona was in her eighties. She lived in a retirement home in Ojai, California, for five years before she came back to Minnesota.

Now her nieces and nephews and their many children

look in on her regularly, celebrate holidays with her, call her on the phone.

"They're my family now and they're very, very precious to me," she says seriously. "One niece feels as if I were her mother. We're very close."

She is around young families enough to have a strong opinion about what's wrong with the American family today.

"I think that women are not taking responsibility for family life as my parents did. My mother had a great deal of influence on my life, and I never could thank her enough for the feeling that she raised me with—the sharing feelings that I have about everybody. I think there's something lacking today. I think it's partly because the mothers' attention has been pulled aside by the suffrage deal and the fact that they can go out and earn a living. And I think our whole country—private life, public life, everything—has swung more to the financial aspect of life, not for the creative and wonderful things that life can offer."

"You think people are too interested in making money?"

"That's right. I think that greed has gotten to the point where it ought to be curbed. I don't know why people should be able to earn—indefinitely—huge amounts that they never, never, never use, to the complete rejection of scattering it so that people everywhere can get some benefit. I think it's too one-sided. Everything is going over to the financial side of the picture and not about what life is for."

"Which is what?"

"Well, it's to share. The big thing in life is to share. Everything. Responsibilities as well as all of the good things.

I think there's a sharing that's not participated in as much as it has formerly been. That's the selfishness of the current age. I mean sharing what you have to offer. Making it count. Because everybody has some of that, you know?"

Mona sighs deeply. She is getting tired. Suddenly I realize that I have not planned this day very well. She's telling me the meaning of life, for goodness sake, and I'm watching the clock. I should have left my schedule completely open. I can't come back tomorrow; I've got a flight reservation to go home. I'm only starting to get a complete sense of her today and she's running out of steam.

I'd resolved to let her talk, and I was good about keeping quiet, but now it's the end of the day, she's tired, and I have a lot more questions.

"Mona, I need to ask you one more thing. If I were to live to be a hundred, what do I have to look forward to? What are the joys of being as old as you are?"

"Well, sometimes I wonder if there *is* joy in it. I'm satisfied to look back on my past and say to myself, 'I think you've lived a good life. Are you happy with it, Mona?' And I say to myself, 'No, there are a lot of things I could have done better, but I didn't know how.' On the other hand, I think I have prevented a lot of worse things happening, and I think, comparing the two things, I have to be satisfied with that. I tried to do my part."

She asks if we can stop. "I'm kinda tired out," she says.

I didn't want to stop. Mona was the first centenarian I'd met who was so lucid, whose memories were so complete, who had a sense of herself in the past and the present. I was just getting to know her and I wanted to just chat with her in a friendly way, to forget about "the interview" for a moment. I turned off the tape recorder and asked if I could see her room before I left.

She called it her cubbyhole. It was like a college dorm room, long and narrow with a single window facing west. It was smaller than an average hotel room. Mona had books and photographs all around, including one taken at her hundredth birthday party in which she wore an olive-green silk dress with a mandarin collar. It was form-fitting and I admired it. She went to the closet, which was stuffed to overflowing, and pulled the dress out to show me. It was draped in a plastic cleaning bag. She lifted the bag and now I have forever this image of her, one arm cradling the shiny green dress, her eyes sparkling, one girl showing her fancy dress to another.

4

ANNA WILMOT

"I tell you, I'm something, aren't I?"

IT'S DECEMBER 1999. Time is running out on the century, and my radio series about centenarians is scheduled to begin in one month. I'm not ready and I'm nervous. All the interviews I've done so far have problems. I've misjudged people's energy, not stayed long enough, and never felt that I had a grasp of an entire life as I've wanted to. I have no vision of the series; I don't know what I want to say. Every time I meet someone, there's a new variable to contend with. I have heard some good stories, but something is missing and I don't know what it is. And worst of all, I'm getting anxious about being confined like a caged animal in my own later years, unable to go where I want.

Then, just before the shortest day of the year, when it's cold, damp, and dark in Washington, my anxiety about the series is compounded by my annual, irrational holiday panic; the tree's not up yet, I don't have matching china for Christmas dinner, I've not mailed any cards *again,* and I've spent way too much money sending presents to my family at the last possible moment because I couldn't plan ahead. I am huddled in front of my full-spectrum light for an hour every morning, to help me fend off depression caused by a lack of sunlight, and I'm wondering where I will get the energy to write this radio series. And at this low moment, I meet three centenarians in one week who give me a new vision of what it means to be one hundred and fill me with hope. They all have a level of independence and passion that I have not encountered. They set me on a path of learning that will change me forever. It begins with Anna Wilmot.

I'D HEARD that Anna rows a boat every day when the weather's warm. I phone her in Massachusetts. She has no trouble using the phone, the first centenarian so far who can deal with it.

"Remember, it's not *Wilmont,* it's *Wilmot,* M-O-T." Anna is instructing me in a voice so energetic I have to pull the receiver away from my ear. "Ask anyone along the road and they'll tell you where Anna lives."

I tell her I'll be there in the morning.

"All right, dear, see you then."

She's calling me "dear" and we haven't met.

I fly to Bradley International Airport just north of Hart-ford and plan to rent a car. I'm the only one on the shuttle bus. The driver is older and calm. The windshield wipers can barely keep up with the sleet. The tension of the weather matches my mood.

A YEAR HAS passed since I interviewed Ella Miller and Mona Breckner, and I've become obsessed with finding out the meaning of life. Mona brought it up and Mrs. Miller radi-ated a wise serenity. I'm carrying in my backpack *The Last Gift of Time: Life Beyond Sixty* by Carolyn G. Heilbrun, a novelist and scholar who's taught English at Columbia University. Heilbrun says she always planned to kill herself when she got to "three score years and ten," but then she "found the revelation that I could look back upon my sixties with pleasure astonishing."

This seems absurd to me, but I keep reading into the night in my cold, king-sized bed with a view of a parking lot and Dumpsters in Springfield, Massachusetts.

The next morning, in the sunniest seat at a Dunkin' Donuts, I'm racing to finish the book before I go to Anna's at ten. I'm hoping that Ms. Heilbrun will try to explain the meaning of life, why she decided to go on. At the end of the last chapter, she quotes the poem "Otherwise" by Jane Kenyon, which I know well because a framed copy of it hangs in my office. The poem articulates the mundane pleasures of Kenyon's daily routine, and looks ahead, knowing it will end someday. To me, it's a poem about enjoying today.

> *At noon I lay down*
> *with my mate. It might*
> *have been otherwise.*
> *We ate dinner together*
> *at a table with silver*
> *candlesticks. It might*
> *have been otherwise.*
> *I slept in a bed*
> *in a room with paintings*
> *on the walls, and*
> *planned another day*

just like this day.
But one day, I know,
it will be otherwise.

"No kidding. I knew *that*. Thanks a lot," I say to Ms. Heilbrun's book, thinking that for a self-described "expensively educated" woman, she hasn't tried very hard.

I'm impatient and I drive too fast toward Anna's house.

She lives outside the small city of Westfield, which calls itself "the buggy-whip capital of the world." I follow her directions down a two-lane highway and then off through the trees toward a lake. The road curves along the shore and then between wooden houses and pine trees. Most of the homes appear to have been built in the twenties and thirties, close to the road. Cars are parked haphazardly, as if parking space was an afterthought. I can imagine kids in flip-flops and bathing suits walking along the sandy road in the summer.

I'm standing on the steps of Anna's home at the end of the road, a one-story wooden cabin surrounded by pine trees. It could use a coat of paint. I'm knocking on the wooden screen door. I bend over to read a small enameled plaque below the screen. It says *F. B. Wilmot* in an elegant script.

"Hang on, I'm comin'," Anna yells from inside.

Anna Wilmot is a blast of color and energy—bright red hair, flushed cheeks, blue eyes, big smile. She's wearing a black sweatshirt that announces *Maui*.

Her kitchen is dark and warm with knotty pine paneling. A row of canes hangs off the edge of the counter next to the door. There's an old white refrigerator with a rounded front, and a vintage stove. A tiny table is against the wall, with a view out the window; clearly it's the place where Anna eats alone and reads.

"Didja have trouble findin' me?"

None whatsoever. Her directions were perfect. She still drives herself.

She leads me into the living room, which is full of light. The house is on a wooded point that juts out into the lake. We're surrounded on three sides by water. It's deeply quiet. A clock ticks. It feels cozy and windswept at the same time.

"I just love it here," she says as she plunks herself into her rocking chair. "You know, at my age, you don't sit down, you plop!"

The room is "a typical home from the 1940s" you could expect to see at the Smithsonian Institution. There's a sofa along one wall, covered in a cotton fabric with a Chinese motif. The hard, thin rug is a flowered wool print, worn in spots. There's a sleeping porch beyond French doors on the left, three small bedrooms on the right. Anna isn't a stickler for home decoration, but everything's neat and clean. It feels a little rough around the edges, which appeals to me. She notices that I'm looking around. "I guess everything here is an antique, just like me!" she laughs.

Anna has a loud, high-pitched, exuberant laugh. It's the first time, I realize, that I've heard a centenarian laugh so freely.

I can tell this is going to be a good day.

ANNA WAS born in Holyoke, Massachusetts, where her father ran a grocery store. They moved around some, to

Westfield and then to Springfield. When they lived in town, they came to this lake in the summers.

Suddenly a voice comes from the kitchen: "Hell-ooooooh."

"Hi, Mr. Sherman," Anna calls out as she pushes herself out of the rocker. I follow her into the kitchen, where there are now some aluminum food containers on the counter. Mr. Sherman is already gone.

"It's my meal," Anna says as she feels them for tempera-ture. "Meals-on-Wheels. It's hot. You wanna eat it? Do you wanna eat now? Aren't you hungry?"

I convince Anna that I can wait and we go back to her family history.

She positions herself in front of my microphone, which she treats respectfully, as if people are waiting to hear us on the radio and she and I are deciding what we'll tell them. It tickles me to see how seriously she takes it.

Soon she tells me that she has outlived all her family members, including her younger brother Louie, who was her protector, she says, even when they were young. He would chaperone her dates and tell her which of her boyfriends he liked and which ones he didn't like.

"When I lost him, which was sorrowful," she says, "I was left alone. Now there's no one left but me, which isn't the happiest thing for anybody, but there's nothing we can do about it. That's life."

Anna has outlived her husband, Frederick, as well. They met when he was just out of the service in World War I.

"I went with him for a couple of years . . . and I had the

one son, Frederick, who lives in California now. I call him my baby; he's seventy-five years old." Anna laughs again.

She tells me the broad outlines of her life. I keep asking her to go back to fill in details and tell stories.

"When you were growing up, what did you do after school?"

"We were outdoor kids. We walked a lot. We used to play hide-and-go-seek, things like that. There was no TV to keep us in the house. We'd take long rides on our bikes. We all loved our bicycles."

She could be describing my own childhood in Indiana in the fifties. We lived in the country and we were always on our bikes.

Anna tells me about the Great Depression, how she and Frederick nearly lost everything, how she learned to be frugal and survive on very little. She is not sad or even wistful. It was hard but she survived. We've been talking for less than two hours when she says, "I think that about covers every-thing."

I agree to stop and have lunch with her, but I'm certain we're not finished.

She talks me into eating her lunch from Meals-on-Wheels, which she proceeds to heat up on her old stove. She blows out a kitchen match and turns up the gas. "I always have enough food in the house," she says. "Believe it or not, I can still cook. I do!"

She jerks the pan back and forth to move the rice and tomato sauce around.

"This stove is an antique. Like me!"

"Anna, you don't look a day over eighty," I say.

"Thank you." She means it. "You know these carnivals where they guess your age? I'd love to do that. Ooooh, this smells good." She moves quickly, shakes the pan again, instructs me to set the table in the living room, and opens the other food containers on the counter.

"Looks like chocolate pudding. You like chocolate pudding? What kinda sandwich we got here? Looks like ham and cheese. Here, you can take this with you when you go. *Take* it. And here's a cookie, too."

I let Anna fuss over me. She comes to the table and sits across from me. "Okay, sweetie pie," she says, "where's your drink?"

We chat easily for an hour over lunch. She keeps jumping up from her chair to show me pictures and letters and birthday cards she received on her hundredth birthday the year before, including a greeting from Willard Scott, who announces centenarians' birthdays on NBC's *Today* show.

The phone rings and apparently someone has died.

"Oh, yes, he was a very nice man," Anna is saying. "Penny, are you going? . . . Well, I wonder if my car will make it. . . . Oh, I'll appreciate that."

She hangs up.

"A friend of ours died and the wake is Sunday. He was a nice man. It's a shame. You know, I have a friend, he's a Baptist and he's always trying to convert me. Anytime he sends me anything, he puts these little reminders inside that say 'Where are you headed?' "

"Where are you headed, Anna?" I ask.

"I don't give it a thought," she says, and that's her last word on the afterlife for now.

I CONVINCE HER that I have a lot more questions and she seems surprised but agrees to sit back down in the rocker. It occurs to me that Anna doesn't care to talk about the past. She's living in the present, making plans for the future. But there's a lot I need to know.

"How old was your husband, Frederick, when he died?"

"He was seventy-eight. Wait, is that right?" She calcu-lates in her head. "Yeah, seventy-eight. I was seventy-two."

"What was it like to be alone suddenly?"

"It was terrible." For the first time today Anna's voice is low and quiet. "It was like my right hand being torn offa me. I knew I had to calm down. I was ready to sell the house and move. I don't know where I was gonna move, but thank good-ness I calmed down and stayed. And I'm glad I did. This is my home and I like it."

"Where were you thinking about going?"

"I didn't know. I thought I had to get out. And away. I was too confused. Too upset. But, as I say, I calmed down, so I didn't have to make a decision."

"You've been alone for thirty years now."

"Yeah, that's a long time. But I hadda go on. I hadda take care of myself. I knew I hadda be healthy and not get sick because there was nobody to care for *me*. I just made it, thank goodness."

"Did you think about the future?"

"No, I was so taken with his death that there was no future. Nothing left. Until I calmed down, and then I just went from day to day. Then it became a way of living. And I accepted it. There was nothing left for me to do." She laughs. "A few years later a few menfolks thought they had an eye for me. But I said, *nothing doing!*"

"You mean somebody wanted to marry you?"

"Who knows what they had in mind, but I didn't give it a chance. I had the best, I didn't want the rest."

I have the sense that Anna has said this a lot.

"Do you still think about your husband?"

"Well, that's part of your life. You can't live with somebody that long and not think about them. We had a very, very good marriage. We got along. We'd argue about things—who doesn't?—but it was nothing serious. Nothing that ever occurred ever really made us angry at each other. The only thing I can say is that we were happy together."

"Did you laugh?"

"Absolutely! He had a good sense of humor and I was pretty good, too."

"A lot of people imagine that when they're your age they'll be lonely."

"I've had a lot of people ask me if I get lonesome. Well, I won't allow myself to get lonesome. I get out and do something about it. I take a walk. *I will not allow myself to get lonesome.*" She proclaims this directly to the microphone and then turns to me and says in a lower voice, "It's true."

"Anna, do you think about your age? In your mind are you older?"

"No, it doesn't bother me. I just hope I never have to go

to a nursing home. I hope I never do. I hope when the time comes I go peacefully, no long illness. Just have it over with."

"Seems like you have folks around you, Anna. You're not alone here."

"That's true. You know, I'm a reader. I like to read in the afternoon. Sometimes when I get interrupted, I'm a little cross, but I forgive them. I did have one neighbor, every little while she was checking up on me. She was so afraid! So, in a decent way, I told her not to fret, that if I did feel I needed her, I'd call. I kind of stopped her from looking in on me constantly. She meant well." She turns to me again and in that lower voice says, "It's true, she had me goin' crazy! I couldn't *do* anything. She was too good." Anna chuckles to herself. "Okay, one more question. I gotta go."

"Anna, what do people have to look forward to, being a hundred years old?"

"Well, the only thing I can say is, Don't sit. Get going. Move. Have an incentive. Don't keep thinking 'I'm old.' Get it out of your system. Keep going! I don't stay put. That's it."

ANNA WILMOT was the first hundred-year-old person I met who lives alone.

She survives on her income from Social Security; her husband had no pension and she has stripped her needs down to a minimum. She can still drive, but she's planning to give up her car soon because the insurance costs so much. Anna's life doesn't range far, but she seems content.

I have a vision of myself living alone in a house like hers fifty years from now, wearing a sweatshirt and sneakers, shaking pans on the stove to heat up my lunch from Meals-on-Wheels, reading books all afternoon, sleeping in a pine-paneled bedroom with a view of water.

Meeting Anna has also helped me confront one of my biggest fears about growing old: the loss of physical activity.

I've always loved to swim and bike and skate and hike and be on the water in a boat. As a teenager, I was consumed with ballet and modern dance, and flirted with the idea of becoming a professional.

I can't imagine life without the rush I feel riding a bike fast downhill, the warmth that heats my brain when I cross-country ski in freezing air, the weightless, flying gracefulness of mind that swimming outdoors induces.

Most days I swim at the YMCA pool near my home, and there, in the locker room, I see the ravages of time on the female body.

Clothing masks a lot of bad alignment and bad luck, but none of us has secrets when we stand side by side in the shower. Crooked spines, lumpy skin, slumping shoulders, pro-truding necks, flabby arms. It's sobering to see the future of my body every day.

I remember once my grandmother Nina took one of our bikes for a spin around the driveway. She hadn't been on a bike in years, she said. I was amazed to see an old lady ride a bike. I thought only kids could have that kind of fun. I figure now she was in her sixties at the time. Not old at all, by my current standards.

When I got older and she was still alive, every time I'd hike in the woods, I'd think, I'm doing this for her—she can't anymore. And now that she's gone, I resolve to never stop.

"COME ON, let's go outside," Anna says.

She puts on her winter coat. I follow her down the steps and across the driveway to the mailbox. She retrieves a few Christmas cards.

"I wanna show you something back here." She grabs a stick, an old shovel handle, and takes off toward the lake, walking carefully on the dry pine needles. "Watch the tree roots," she instructs me.

"See, there's my boat." She points the stick at a wooden, flat-bottom rowboat, upside down by the shore.

"That's where I go, down there. Look at how nice and calm the water is. If I had known it was gonna be like this, I would have left the boat in."

She continues around back and sits down on some steps that come out from the porch.

"See, I come out here, just like this, and I sit in the sun. Isn't this nice?"

We're looking out across the lake, toward the west. The tree branches hang low over the water here on the point and the late-afternoon sun pours melted gold on Anna's world. Her red hair is brilliant. A light comes out of her.

"And when you get out here, there's no interference, nobody around. You can come out here and you can skinny-dip."

"What?"

"I do! But only if it's foggy and there's no fishermen around."

She reaches over and puts her hand on top of my microphone, laughing loudly. She doesn't want our listeners to hear her skinny-dipping story, which includes the use of the word *hinder*. Finally she takes her hand off the microphone and continues.

"Oh, I could write a book. I just love it here."

I TAKE ANNA'S picture and she takes mine. Later I send copies to her son, Freddie, her "baby," in California, and in return he sends me a one-pound package full of family photos and newspaper clippings. There's Anna as a young girl with a long ponytail, as a teenager with her basketball team, a newlywed looking mischievous with Frederick, photos from all of Anna's life, up to the present. In picture after picture, there's the lake, too. Here she is rolling down her stockings, getting ready to swim. And here, with a girlfriend, their knees drawn up to their chests, sitting on a dock, in long, wool bathing suits and rubber caps. And here she is with Frederick, in middle age, dressed up for a fancy occasion, both of them wearing white shoes, laughing and sitting together on the bumper of a black sedan, the lake visible through the trees behind them.

Anna chose to live here, on this lake, when her husband died, even though Freddie begged her to come and live with him in California. She knew herself well enough to know what would sustain her and give her life meaning. I don't feel as if I have to ask her the meaning of life.

"I don't want to die," she says. "I want to stay here. And you know, I'm *gonna* stay here. I want them to throw my ashes in the pond, so I'm warning all the neighbors: 'Don't eat the fish, they might be eatin' me!'" We both laugh hard. "I tell you, I'm something, aren't I?"

5

ABRAHAM GOLDSTEIN

"You don't live in the past,
you live in the present."

"ABRAHAM GOLDSTEIN," said the handwritten note, "Professor—Baruch College—age 99—supposed to be amazing." A friend made a speech in New York City two years ago and mentioned my search for centenarians. A woman in the audience gave her this name. I've saved the note.

Now I'm waiting in the professor's office, looking for clues. What kind of man still goes to work at age 101? A plaque on the wall says, "In appreciation of your sixty years as an outstanding educator, friend and colleague. Baruch College Law Department. March 1989." He's been teaching *seventy* years. There are no other mementos, photographs, or awards, no artwork, nothing personal. It's a concrete-block room with fluorescent lights and a cold tile floor.

The door opens and he appears in silence, wearing a single-breasted raincoat and a fedora the same golden brown color. He's carrying an umbrella and wearing rubbers on his shoes.

He gives me a stare.

"Hi! I'm the reporter!" I chirp.

"Oh," he says dryly. Instantly, I am nervous.

He takes off his coat and hat. He's wearing a brown polyester blazer and brown pants, a blue oxford-cloth shirt, a beige sweater vest, and a striped tie. His hair is silvery white, full and wavy on top. He's wearing fifties glasses, back in style again. He shakes my hand gently. His hands are smooth and slender. He has a mild and thoughtful expression. He moves easily to the back of the office, opens a high filing cabinet drawer, pulls out a two-inch-thick paperback textbook, and thuds it down on the desk.

I start firing questions at him, each one unrelated to the one before, which is what I do when I'm nervous.

"What's your assignment for today?" I begin.

"I understand a student was scheduled for twelve o'clock. So far nobody showed up," he says cheerfully.

Professor Goldstein is retired from the classroom. Now he has two primary responsibilities. One is tutoring. Today he's expecting three students, one each hour. It's the week of final exams here at Baruch's Zicklin School of Business on Park Avenue South. Professor Goldstein tutors the law of contracts. He could do it in his sleep.

His other responsibility is to prepare briefs for his colleagues about recent rulings that affect business law in the state of New York. In other words, he keeps them up-to-date.

Before I can really dig into anything, a student enters. Her name is Muriel. Her demeanor is demure but her outfit is hot: skintight leather pants, body-hugging pullover, and a black chenille cap pulled down to the eyebrows over long, shiny black ringlets. She looks sexy and tough but her voice is earnest and sweet.

"I didn't know this was going to be a one-on-one session. I thought it was a class," she says quietly.

"What's that?" the professor says.

"Do I have to sign an attendance sheet?"

"You have to speak loudly, my hearing's not too good."

"Do I have to sign an attendance sheet?"

"What's that? Speak up!"

"DO I HAVE TO SIGN AN ATTENDANCE SHEET?"

"No, just tell me what your problem is . . . and for fifty cents, I'll give you the answers." He's grinning.

She giggles.

"Of course, they won't be the correct answers."

She moves around the desk to be closer to the professor. He's forgotten his hearing aids today. They sit close. She has the textbook spread flat on her lap and the page is heavily highlighted, but she seems bewildered and fumbles around in her book until she comes to a topic she's fuzzy about: the violation of statutes.

"What page are you on?" he asks.

"Page one fifty-six."

"Page one fifty-four?"

"Fifty-SIX."

"Page one fifty-six?" He's leafing through his book. "There is no page one fifty-six."

She giggles again. When he gets to the page, he glances at the heading and throws a switch in his mind.

"Bribery in New York State, as in most states, is a crime," he begins. "So, for example, if Alice enters into an agreement with B . . ."

For ten minutes, without taking his eyes from her face, he explains, firmly and gently. When he's finished, Muriel still has a blank look and she hasn't taken any notes.

"Are you gonna remember all this?" he asks. "You might want to take some notes." He is gentle.

She mumbles something about remembering and absentmindedly turns more pages in her book. The professor is not judgmental. He is silent and motionless, his eyes on her. He's got as much time as she wants.

"In an exam . . ." she starts.

"I can't hear you," he says.

"IN AN EXAM . . ." she starts again. They go on for another twenty minutes, doing an odd kind of mind dance: She halfheartedly asks a few more unfocused questions and he answers, sometimes not quite hearing what she's said and giving an answer to a question she did not ask. I want to interrupt and say, "No, no, that's not what she meant," but I don't. Somehow they end up in the same place together.

She tells him she's not prepared and he says, "That's okay, take your time," so, perhaps not wanting to offend him, she keeps leafing through her book, hoping she'll find a concrete question. He patiently watches.

Finally she says softly, "I think that's all the questions I have. Thank you very much."

"Are you sure?" he says.

She nods.

"Now, make sure to read every word in the questions on the exam."

She nods and thanks the professor timidly but respectfully and leaves, closing the door behind her.

"Professor, can I ask you about your early life?" I say in a loud voice.

"I didn't have an early life," he deadpans, and now I'm giggling.

"I understand that as a young teenager you were a messenger boy."

"Who told you that?"

Goldstein has been the subject of a number of newspaper articles.

"I was born in Meriden, Connecticut, and we moved to Bridgeport when I was thirteen."

That would have been around 1910, before child labor laws were enacted. Being a messenger could be dangerous then, especially at night. The professor says he worked after school from five to eleven.

"There were a couple of streets in Bridgeport that were solely houses of prostitution. They were very good calls because they were very generous with their tips. I suppose they thought, Easy come, easy go. They'd call a messenger to mail a letter. I was only a kid then, about fifteen. Well, one night, the madam opened the door and this girl comes from upstairs and all she had on was a kimono and the kimono opens wide and there I am with my mouth open."

He laughs easily at the memory.

"I was just a kid, you see? But, as I say, they were very good calls. I delivered a baby once, too. A woman was ill, she had me deliver the baby to the grandma. She had that baby wrapped up in so many blankets, it couldn't have gotten hurt if I dropped it. There were different jobs like that. It wasn't easy, but the family needed the money."

Goldstein's parents were Russian Jewish immigrants. His father was a tailor. He remembers that when he was a kid, he was crazy about baseball, but his father would say, "Let me see you with a book in your hand." He was an obedient son.

A lot of the students at Baruch College are the children

of immigrants, too, working to put themselves through school just like he did, so he empathizes with their struggling.

Another young woman arrives. This one is tall and Twiggy-thin with heavily coated eyelashes, blond hair pulled back hard into a stumpy ponytail. Her name is Anna.

She comes around behind the desk and sits beside him, too.

"You got lunch for me there?" he teases.

"No, I'm sorry," she says, smiling back.

"I'll wait till you bring it." He's twinkling at her.

"I hear you are great," she says earnestly, hands in her lap, "and that you really know the law of contracts."

He misses the compliment.

"The law of contracts?" He holds his hand up to his ear. "I'm having a little trouble understanding. There are different types of law. The law of contracts is a separate kind."

Anna follows his lead. She has questions prepared.

"I don't understand, when a contract is modified . . ." she begins.

"What page are you on?"

She looks down at the book in her lap. "Page one forty-two."

"There is no page one forty-two!"

"There must be!" She's giggling now.

The professor seems pleased that she is prepared and moves directly into the moment with her. "Now, consideration is needed for all types of contracts. . . ."

She listens carefully and takes notes in a looping script. He watches her write and keeps talking. Now and then he'll quiz her, and when she answers correctly, his eyebrows fly up and he nods excitedly, saying, "That's *right*."

It's pleasing to watch the two of them. He is enjoying the connection with this eager, unguarded woman. They go on for nearly an hour until Anna says she has no more questions. The professor delivers his admonition to pay attention to every word in the exam questions.

"The words are there for a reason," he says. "Now, are you gonna remember all that?"

"I'll remember." She nods.

"I'm gonna call you at three o'clock in the morning to ask you questions," he jokes.

"I hear you've been teaching seventy years," she says. "You must love it. Wow. That's great."

"Yeah, and when I get home I fall down," he says.

When she's gone, I start in with my own questions again. I have some hopes of getting a glimpse of New York in the early part of the century.

"Do you remember when the Empire State Building went up?"

"I have no recollection of that."

"Do you remember when you got your first radio?"

"No, I have no idea."

"Did you ever see Babe Ruth play baseball?"

"No, I used to read about him in the paper. Couldn't afford to go to baseball games."

"Do you remember when the stock market crashed?"

"No, I have no recollection of it."

"Can you tell me about the Depression?"

"That was a tough period. I was fortunate to have a job."

I think to myself, Aha! We're on to something.

He continues. "In those days, I had to send money home. It was very difficult."

"Sending money to your brothers and sisters in Connecticut?"

He nods. "I knew they would manage somehow, but I wanted to make it easier for them." He was teaching and working full-time then. "It wasn't easy, but it paid off."

"Professor, when you were twenty years old, what did you think your life was going to be like?"

He laughs thoughtfully. "I didn't think I had time to think about it, between school and work. I had to work full-time and went to evening sessions for seven years, college and then law school. I had a job and homework. I had to do homework on the weekends. But I have no regrets."

The way he phrases the answer—"I didn't think I had time to think about it"—makes me wonder if he's saying that he would have done things differently. And when someone tells me so emphatically that they have no regrets, it seems like a tip-off.

"Professor, what's your day like when you're not here in the office?"

His voice softens. "You'd be surprised how time passes. Mostly reading. This takes a lot of my time." He lifts a copy of the annual review of business law cases he prepares for his colleagues. "I do this at home, at night. Sometimes I forget what time it is. I'll wonder why I'm sleepy and realize it's three in the morning. You get busy and you don't realize the time."

"Do you live alone?"

"Yeah," he says quietly.

"Do you get out and walk?"

"I try and walk about a mile a day. If you don't, you know, your muscles waste away. Same thing with the mind. If you don't use it, it wastes away."

"Do you read the paper?"

"Yeah."

"*Times?*"

"*Post,* mostly. I like their columns. I pick up the *Times* now and then to see what I'm missing." He grins.

"You never married?"

"No. . . ."

"You've lived alone this whole time?"

"I've never permitted myself to get entangled. I had problems at home with my sisters and brothers and I had to help them financially. I felt if I got married, I wouldn't be able to do it. I think it was a mistake. I think they would have managed without me."

So there is some regret.

I don't know the professor well enough to say if living alone has been sad for him. Was there ever someone he loved? Someone not available to him? Or was caring for his siblings the only reason he never got "entangled"? And if so, were they aware of his sacrifice? He isn't about to tell me these things here, in his office, between tutoring appointments, and he has refused my request to do this interview at his home. He wants me at arm's length. Fair enough. He's done a lot of interviews lately and I can tell he doesn't enjoy talking about being one hundred years old. And why should he tell me about his personal life?

"Does it seem silly to you that people care that you're one hundred years old?"

"Not silly, but I don't care for it. It's just another day. It's like walking ten miles, a step at a time, living and breathing, one day at a time, one week at a time. Before you know it, you're a hundred years old. The body doesn't function, of course. You know, some young girls gave me a seat on the bus. I was flattered. I thought, I must be handsome, but I got some pictures they took here recently and I see that's not the reason." He smiles.

He's not hostile about it, or even defensive, he just doesn't see good reasons to dwell on the past.

"What's the point?" he says. "You don't live in the past, you live in the present and, if possible, in the future. Unless you bring up the past, you don't think about it."

A THIRD STUDENT arrives for his tutoring session. His name is David. He's got a stubbly beard and a serious slouch. He's in deep trouble. His exam is in two days and he's barely familiar enough with the material to form a logical question.

"What about performance?" he asks the professor.

"What?"

"Performance outside of one year."

"So, what about it?" For the first time today, the professor shows impatience.

"When does the agreement begin?" asks David.

"What kind of contract are you talking about? It depends on what you're talking about," says the professor.

They go on like this for a few minutes. David doesn't

understand his own questions, so he can't know if he's getting an answer he can use. Suddenly he looks over at me and
lowers his voice.

"What station will this be on?"

"On public radio, nationwide."

"Do you make a lot of money doing this?"

"Not really. But I like it."

"Me, I'm trying to get into acting."

"Not business?"

"No, it's too strict an environment. . . . I don't know . . .
we'll see where fate takes me." He gives me a grin. He's still
wearing his winter coat and his baseball cap is turned back-
ward on his head. I am suddenly embarrassed that we are con-
versing too quietly for the professor to hear. I glance at him
and he is looking directly at David, waiting patiently for him.

David looks up, too, and the professor says, "Is that it?"

"I guess so."

"Good luck on the exam. Who's your professor?"

"Graulich."

"Good professor."

"Not as smart as you."

"Of course not." Goldstein grins.

"Not as good-looking, either." David makes the most of
the show of goodwill.

"And not as young as I am."

"Can I go?"

"You can go."

"Thank you, Your Honor."

"Okay, good luck." He waves David off, shaking his head
with an exasperated smile.

"Professor, do you need to take a break?" I start up again.

"No. You're nosy." He's smiling, though, and we chat for a while longer. He shows no sign of impatience with me, but he doesn't tell me stories, either. He is far less interested in talking about himself than he is in being with the students. I get glimpses of his life, short anecdotes, but little context or background. I've been with him half a day and I give up.

"What about you, do you have children?" This comes out of the blue.

"No, just me and my husband." This question flusters me. "We travel a lot."

"Other people manage," he says flatly.

His words sting. "I guess they do."

I'VE CONCLUDED that despite his sweet nature and amiability, Professor Goldstein never wanted to take this interview as far as I did. He's ready for me to be gone and so I leave.

Outside it's dark and cold. An early-winter rainstorm has lasted all day. I feel so bad that I decide to walk, even though I'm not dressed for the weather. I roll my equipment bag down the street, west of Baruch College toward Madison Square. The puddles are ankle deep in low spots but I plod through, between empty park benches, as heavy raindrops pop on the surface of the water all around. My umbrella is too small, my back is wet, my gloves are soaked. The sidewalk curves and I follow, arguing with myself about how I could have done a better interview, wondering why I couldn't connect with him, and puzzled by his comment "Other people manage." I took it as a criticism, no doubt an overreaction.

I continue toward Chelsea and imagine the professor on the bus now, briefcase on his lap, headed for home. Later he'll sit in his chair in a pool of light, with a yellow legal pad by his side, immersed in the present moment, doing the work he loves. I look up and the cool, white triangle of the Flatiron Building bursts before me, singing with strength, and I am suddenly moved back in time. A dark, wet team of horses approaches from my left, squeaking leather, hoofs splashing, horsey smells, and a driver in a top hat passes me at the curb. And following behind, a hunched figure on a bicycle, leather pouch slung over his shoulder, a rooster tail of spray rising from the rear tire. It's a young, pale, slender messenger boy, eyes focused far ahead.

6

MARGARET RAWSON

"We used to go out into the park in back and eat lunch."

MARGARET RAWSON was the third centenarian that week who changed my life.

She lives in a two-hundred-year-old farmhouse called Foxes Spy on a winding country road near Frederick, Maryland. A soft-spoken young woman named Charlotte Chamberlain meets me at the back door, takes my coat, and offers me a hot drink. The kitchen is cozy, with a low ceiling, well-worn, handmade wooden cabinets, and a boxlike refrigerator with a coil on top. It's from 1928, Charlotte says, and still works fine. There's an old, brown Crosley Bakelite radio on a shelf, too, and the faint smell of woodsmoke.

Charlotte leads me toward the living room and we pass through what was once a large foyer, now converted to a home office. There's a seated elevator mounted alongside the stairs, a Macintosh computer, a Kurzweil reading machine, and a color enlarger, too. We walk across wooden floorboards twelve inches wide and Persian carpets with their edges secured to the floor with duct tape. A coffee table holds stacks of recorded books.

Margaret comes in, leaning over her walker, taking tiny steps. Her hair is wavy and white, cut sensibly short, a silver headband holding it off her round and pale face. She smiles easily, meets my eyes directly, and takes my hand in both of hers.

Charlotte helps her find a comfortable position in just the right chair, and I clip a tiny lavalier microphone to her sweater. I put on headphones and hear a roaring as the furnace fan cycles on. Margaret instructs Charlotte to switch it off and asks her who will be arriving on the next shift. Margaret has three caregivers, each one for eight hours at a time. "It's my support group," she laughs. Charlotte leans over and kisses Margaret on the lips. "See you tomorrow," she says.

She wants to know about my project and I answer, but I'm distracted by her physical problems. Her body is so weak and slack. Her shoulders slump. Her hands shake.

"What's it like to adjust to moving so slowly?" I ask.

"You just move more slowly," she says. "I dream about walking just like everybody and then I wake up and find I can't. The other night I dreamed I was walking across the room and my legs gave out."

"Do you dream about being younger?"

"Yes, quite often. But you wanted to talk about my dyslexia work, didn't you?"

She doesn't want to talk about her failing body, she wants to talk about her work. I have been gently reminded that I am focused on her weakness and not her strength.

Margaret Rawson is an expert on dyslexia and her work is known around the world. Dyslexia is a language-based disability. Dyslexics have trouble recognizing and comprehending written language. In the 1920s, as the librarian at a progressive school in Rose Valley, Pennsylvania, she encountered dyslexia for the first time. In those days, very few people knew what it was. Determined to help the students, she learned everything there was to know about it and made it her mission to spread the word that dyslexics could be helped. At age ninety-six, she published *Dyslexia over the Lifespan,* a fifty-five-year study of some of those first students. It showed that they had done just as well in their careers—in some cases better—than the general population because they'd had the right kind of reading instruction.

Today dyslexia is much better understood, thanks in large part to Margaret Rawson. Special schools have been created as her legacy, academic prizes have been given in her name, trees planted in her honor.

I know very little about the specifics of her work, though, so she gives me her books and invites me to come back. We spend the rest of the day talking about her past.

MARGARET BYRD RAWSON was born in 1899 in Rome, Georgia. Her father was a newspaper editor for a while and then made his way to Costa Rica to raise bananas. Her mother died when she was a baby, so she was raised by her mother's parents, who were Quakers in Philadelphia. She remembers her grandmother as generous and wise.

"On the first day of first grade, my grandmother said, 'You're going to college. I know just where you're going and you're going to do good work.'" Margaret says this with wonder and not pride. Her grandmother was the major influence on her life.

"My grandmother was very proud of her grandfather, who'd been a colonel in Washington's army."

"Your grandmother had stories about George Washington?" I ask.

"She told me quite a few."

The stories include a two-hundred-year-old joke about General Washington and the British that involves an out-house, but she asks me not to repeat it.

"My grandmother still hated the English," she says. "She also hated Southerners, but she did not prejudice me against my father's people."

The Southern relatives owned land and slaves.

"Five hundred slaves—a whole village," she says. "My grandmother would go around the plantation with a big ring of keys, ministering to all the people that worked there, seeing they had the medicine they needed. That sort of thing.

"My grandfather left home to join the Confederate army," she says. "He took a horse and a slave and came back without the horse and without the slave and with only four of the fingers on one of his hands."

She speaks slowly and carefully. No word is wasted. But her voice is weak. She can barely project it. She coughs and asks to take a break. I unclip her microphone and help her stand. She takes her walker and heads for the bathroom.

It's quiet in the house. More than an hour has passed since we started. I can hear a clock ticking and realize it's taken me this long to slow myself down to her pace, to stop my racing mind and just listen to what she's saying.

Twenty minutes later she returns and settles in to tell me about a job she had in Philadelphia, one of many that helped her pay her college tuition. She was working for the publishers of the *Saturday Evening Post,* one of the country's most respected magazines.

"I wrote letters to small boys who had subscribers that

they delivered to. And they had huge accounts—like fifteen or twenty-five cents—and they would make an error of three cents." She laughs. "The carriers were just little boys and I had to write them a letter." She pauses to cough again, and with her next words, I feel a perceptual shift; there is a silent click in my mind. The words themselves are oddly inconsequential, but they conjure a vivid scene. I can see and hear and smell it as if I am there. "We had an interesting group of young women who were working in that place, and we got ourselves together as a club and we used to do things together. Our office was near Independence Hall, and we used to go out into the park in back and eat lunch."

I can see those girls sitting on the grass in full skirts, their long hair swept up. Robins hop in the cool spring grass and horses clop on the cobblestone street.

I am all listening and no thinking. It's a good feeling. In my journal later I described it as "falling." I said I had fallen into that moment with her. I didn't consult my list of historic events and I didn't worry about the time. I just gave myself to her and let her take me where she wanted to go.

I am sitting close to Margaret on a low stool at her feet so her weak eyes can see my face. Her eye contact is direct and even sometimes piercing. Mostly her face is expressionless, but now and then she raises her eyebrows and leans toward me, just as I saw Professor Goldstein do with his students, and when that happens, I get a glimpse of a young woman and I feel the fiery, insatiable curiosity she still has.

She goes on and on, talking about her work and the outer limits of her own knowledge of how the human brain works. She tells me about recent breakthroughs in neurology that could lead to a better understanding of dyslexia. "We need to know more about how the brain works at the microscopic level," she says, "how the neurons and synapses work."

I'm trailing along now, mostly ignorant about the human brain, but captivated by her passion. She doesn't seem to care that I bring nothing to this conversation but my curiosity. She doesn't care if my questions are silly. She believes that we all need to open our minds, that we can learn at any age. She is a scientist with an optimistic heart.

"The human child has a long childhood," she says. "From before his birth to the time he is fully adult, he is learning to process things and his brain is still changing. I think you can put this in cosmological terms and you can say that by the time man's brain has developed to the point that it can understand the nature of the world, it will be able to process it." We've wandered into a discussion about the fate of humankind.

"Do you mean that the brain is evolving to the point where someday human beings will be able to understand the complexities of the world better?"

"Yes, we'll be able to see connections and derive meaning from things that we maybe now don't understand, that we're not able to comprehend. The brain is a progressive animal and it takes in more and more of the world and of nature, cosmology, the universe—finer and finer particles of the universe. Somebody once said, 'You've got to know more about everything, but you'll have to narrow your vision until after a while you've examined things so tiny that pretty soon you'll know more and more about less and less until pretty soon you'll know everything about nothing.'" She laughs but she means it. The human brain is striving toward some kind of perfection, she says.

OUR CONVERSATION shakes loose a memory for me.

I am eleven years old, standing alone on the riverbank in the woods behind our house. It's autumn and I am looking at the water flowing from my left to right, downstream.

The river is green; there is a fallen log across it and maple leaves float under it, yellow and red, their edges curled up. I know at this moment that life doesn't get any better. I'm happy. I don't know yet that I will die or that my parents will die. I have a brother and a sister and four grandparents. I have a peaceful and wise feeling. I see an order in the world and I am part of it. For a moment, everything is perfect.

MARGARET AND I talked until the room grew dark and cool, and when I noticed her shivering, I remembered that we had turned off the furnace hours before, to make the room more quiet.

"I think it's time for me to stop," she said.

She had given me a lot to think about.

I was impressed with the way she dealt with her failing body. She got herself the help she needed so that she could do what she wanted. In her condition, Margaret could easily have given up on life, but she was making plans for the future, planning to attend the next national conference of the American Dyslexia Association the following fall.

But as much as I admired her drive and professional

accomplishments, I was intrigued with that "falling" sensation I'd felt. It seemed to happen when I was most relaxed and listening best. I completely lost track of the direction of the conversation, which makes me a little uneasy as a journalist, but I wanted it to happen again.

TWO WEEKS LATER, on New Year's Eve 1999, my husband, Noah, and I went to the Washington National Cathedral to be with the crowds. We didn't go inside for the prayer service but instead went to the lawn overlooking the Mall and the Washington Monument, about three miles away. Fireworks would begin at midnight.

Families were clustered together in the cold. The grandparents were thoughtful, the parents were watching over the children, and the family dogs were squirming on their leashes, unclear about what was happening, but happy to be included. I realized that at least one child in the crowd could be alive a hundred years from tonight. And maybe that child would come back to this place under these same trees to celebrate the coming of the year 2100.

The crowd began chanting—*"Ten! Nine! Eight!"*—I wondered which child it might be—*"Seven! Six! Five!"*—I held my husband's hand, knowing we would both be gone from the earth by then. *"Four! Three! Two!"*—I felt a surge of love for him and for this cold night air and these glorious bells pealing over and over and over, the sound rising and floating out over the city like a flock of doves. Then *"One!"* as the fireworks began.

7

HARRY SHAPIRO

"Shapiro was here."

IT'S JANUARY 2000 and it's too warm in Washington. We haven't had a snowy winter in a few years, so Noah and I head to Maine for a week of skating and walking in cold air. We rent a small cabin by the water that turns out to be a former boathouse, and it's so cold inside that the woodstove has to be stoked all night.

Our trip is also a celebration because my series is launched on NPR and I'm not nervous anymore. I've met hundred-year-old people in great shape, and there are more of them than I'd expected.

And I've been in touch with the authors of the New England Centenarian Study, which published its early findings in 1999. "Growing older does not necessarily mean growing sicker," they've written in *Living to 100*. It could be that as many as fifteen percent of centenarians are still living independently—like Anna, the professor, and Margaret.

I've changed the focus of my series. What began as an American history project is now a personal search for ways of living well. I am still collecting memories, but also strategies.

As we walk late at night in the town of Castine, nearly an island in the Penobscot Bay, there are no people, no cars, no cats or birds. The white clapboard homes lining the streets that lead down to the water are mostly dark. Some have big round thermometers hanging in the front window so the winter caretakers can see if the heat is still on.

We walk fast in the middle of the street, holding our hands in front of our mouths and noses, afraid we have taken too long a route, that we'll be found frozen dead in a ditch by morning. There's no gas station here, no 7-Eleven, no late-night bar.

In the north in winter you remember you're on a planet hurtling through dark space. Moonlight glows bluish on the snow and your eyes are drawn upward. The Milky Way is a wispy banner undulating from horizon to horizon. You could be lifted away into the sky and no one would remember you.

FEBRUARY IN midtown Manhattan. It's blustery on the east/west streets as wind roars off the Hudson River. I duck into the subway. My nose is running, I'm fumbling for coins in my pockets with gloves on, wresting the equipment bag out of a turnstile, trying to read my map without my glasses. I would make a lousy New Yorker.

Finally I find the right platform and settle in for a long ride on the A train to Washington Heights. I'm going to see Harry Shapiro, whom I found in *Life* magazine.

Don't trust photographs of centenarians, I've learned. Old people look impossibly old in them. *Life* has printed a nearly life-size photo of Mr. Shapiro's face. He has unruly eyebrows, age spots on his forehead, vertical drapes of skin under his chin, deep eye sockets. His cheeks are peppered with stubble. There's a lot to look at. But in person, I'd never guess that he's one hundred years old.

Mr. Shapiro gives me "the stare" when I arrive at his apartment. I get it from all the centenarians. They stare like children at first. I finally figured out it's because they can't see or hear well, so I've learned to just stay calm and allow myself to be examined. And I'm staring, too, sizing them up. How well can they see and hear? Can they move around well? Who else is here? Will it be quiet enough for the recording?

A younger woman named Leila takes my coat. Harry Shapiro stands squarely before me. He's shorter than I am, his hair is combed straight back, it's mostly dark. He's wearing a blue button-down shirt, navy cotton trousers, a trim, smooth burgundy sweater vest, and house slippers. He wears no glasses and has a close-trimmed mustache. He shakes my hand. At first he doesn't smile.

Shapiro is a painter and his living room is his gallery. As he stands in the dimly lit foyer, I see behind him oil paintings high and low on the wall, as well as his wife, Celia, in a chair, waiting eagerly to shake my hand. She has a high forehead and snowy hair swept off her face. She carries herself with dignity, even sitting down. The Shapiros are a handsome couple.

Mr. Shapiro pulls up a chair for me in the center of the room. I ask him to sit close and he does, without self-consciousness. I clip a microphone onto his shirt, and realizing that he favors his right ear, I lean close and we begin. He is soon smiling.

"When I came to this country, I was Aaron Shapiro," he says. "I told the teacher, 'I'm Aaron Shapiro,' and she said, 'Well, now you're Harry Shapiro,' and I remained Harry for the rest of my days."

He talks about himself in the past tense.

"My mother brought two little boys to this country. I was five and a half years old."

His father had come ahead of the family, from Pinsk, Russia.

"I was scared stiff of the tall buildings. I said, 'These buildings are going to fall down.' I had never seen more than a three-story building."

These early memories sound practiced to me. He's told them many times but he is enjoying the telling again.

His family settled on the Lower East Side of Manhattan, a city of immigrants unto itself, but soon they moved across the river to Brooklyn, where his father worked as a tailor and Harry went to P.S. 109.

"In the seventh grade, Miss Quimby says, 'We're gonna study the Civil War, children. Does anyone know anything about the Civil War?' My hand went up. 'Harry Shapiro, what do you know about the Civil War?' And I began to talk about the Civil War, began to talk about Manassas, Bull Run, Shiloh, and all the battlefields, and when I got through, after fifteen minutes, she went, 'Harry Shapiro, Harry Shapiro, HARRY SHAPIRO!'" He claps his hands together, as she must have. "'Where did you pick all this up?' I said, 'Well, Miss Quimby, I read about this war. I started two years ago. I'd go to the library and pick up books about the Civil War.'"

When Harry was a boy, the Civil War was only forty years past. He remembers seeing the veterans marching in the Fourth of July parades.

"They *thrilled* me," he says, his voice rising with emotion, but when World War I came along, Harry was too young to serve. Instead he signed up at the Cooper Union for the

Advancement of Science and Art, took classes at night, and went to work drawing women's clothing for catalog companies. He had begun painting, too. He made a studio in his father's basement.

"My father said, 'Harry, who is this guy Picasso? I saw a story about him in the Jewish paper.' I said, 'He's the greatest artist alive.'"

Harry fell in love with the arts, but he was also dutiful and practical. He met Celia, they started a family, and he continued to work at the catalogs.

"Did you like that work?"

He shrugs. "I had to make a living. I ate at two tables, commercial art and fine art." Art was food for him.

"Saturday was my day off," he says. "I used to go to exhibitions of other painters. I was making notes."

By the time the Second World War came along, Harry was too old to serve. One day, in Manhattan during the war, he was on a bus stopped in front of B. Altman and Company, a department store.

"I saw about fifteen blind officers being led into Altman's," he says, and stops abruptly. For a moment I don't know why and then I realize he is pressing his lips together hard to keep from crying out loud. After a long, awkward moment, he says hoarsely, "Three of my friends died in the war."

Celia quickly fills the silence, to relieve his sudden anguish. She speaks in a loud voice from behind me. She is eager to tell me how much she admires her husband. I turn to face her.

"Whatever he did, he used to come and tell me and we would discuss it. If I didn't agree, I would tell him. That's what I liked about that man: He was a thinking man. He's not a man who came home, took the paper, and fell asleep. You talked about everything." She laughs loudly; it's a slightly loony, melodious, rising laugh.

"Tell me, Neenah, would you like to have lunch with us?"

There is a clanging of pots and pans coming from the kitchen. I am given a seat at the table between Harry and Celia. Leila puts out bowls of matzoh ball soup, bagels and whitefish spread, and glasses of juice. Harry and Celia eat eagerly and silently, their heads bowed over their food. I marvel that I have been in this apartment just over two hours and here I am eating at their table as if I did it every day. I feel comfortable, as if I were at my grandmother's.

We eat without speaking much and Leila clears the dishes.

"Neenah," Celia asks, "do you have children?"

"No, I don't."

"Well, you're still young." I don't know if she can tell that I'm forty-five.

Harry gets up from the table and says, "I'd like to show you some paintings," and leads me back to the living room. He takes an art book from its place on a shelf next to his chair, spreads it open on his lap, and starts to leaf through the heavy, shiny pages slowly, reverently.

"My favorite painter is Paul Cézanne," he says, his eyes on the book. "To me, he was the greatest painter of the modern period. He put art on its modern course. He affected me."

"What about it?"

"His color, his design, everything. Do you know that one of his paintings sold for sixty million dollars? Oh, I shouldn't do that—it's a great work of art even if it sold for sixty dollars. Here, this is what I love about his work." He stops to admire an image; his fingers stroke the page lightly. He comes to a portrait.

"That's his wife. She used to bawl him out."

Celia laughs from across the room.

"There he is, the old man himself," Harry says quietly. "That's Cézanne."

Emotion is rising in his throat again and he pauses to let it pass. He turns the page.

"Here's a marvelous painting, two people playing cards. Oh, what a magnificent painting that is, a wonderful rendering. Look at the way he's painted the jackets, the quality of the paints; it's the rebirth of art in a great sense. I want to show you another painting that I love."

He continues turning the pages tenderly.

"This is my favorite Cézanne, a young Italian girl. Look at the way she's in this pensive mood."

"You speak with great love," I say. "It seems that you feel you know Cézanne."

"This man was a beautiful painter, full of poetry and charm. Cézanne has fire in his blood. Color, design—he had it all and it came late in life to him, in the last six or seven years of his life."

"What period of your life have *you* painted the best?"

"Right now."

"You're getting better and better?"

"Yeah. I want to show you one I made. You want to see it in the studio?"

We move to a back bedroom, Harry's studio. It has a bare wooden floor. In one corner, by a window, he has a small desk where he sketches. There are paintings on all the walls. Portraits, mostly, and bucolic tableaux with human figures in them. I recognized the same muted hues of Cézanne. There is a painting-in-progress on an easel. A woman plays a violin, her bowing arm crooked. Beside her is a child in short pants and a pale pink sleeveless shirt. Their feet are hidden in soft grass. Behind them is a flowering bush and a red bird is perched on a branch. The sky is spring blue. It's a quiet painting. He explains that it was inspired by Bach.

He moves along, narrating the walls, showing me other sketches and more paintings: a portrait of Celia's parents, General Hancock with a bold mustache—he was "wounded in the Civil War," he says seriously. We come to the face of a stately woman with a warm, olive complexion and a direct look.

"That's a Roman empress. I saw a lady on the subway one day and I thought she looked like a Roman empress. I couldn't wait to come home and paint her."

The stranger's face stirred something in Harry Shapiro fifty years ago and still does today. He has immortalized a stranger. The mystery he created brings him pleasure.

"Why has it been so important to you to be a painter?"

"It doesn't transcend being a father, but to be a painter is to realize a spiritual portion of life. The ability to put things together and make a whole out of visual and spiritual experiences. What have you seen? What have you heard? I found that there's a thirst for longevity; you want to leave a message for those who come after. 'Papa was here. Grandpa was here.

He felt this about his children.' Autobiography, that's what it is. 'Shapiro was here.'"

BACK IN THE living room, the late-afternoon winter sun is streaming in the windows behind him. The modest size of the apartment is irrelevant to him, it seems. His life has been about ideas and a spiritual search. He has his paintings, his books. He's proud of his daughters and loves his wife. But he remains restless.

"I'd like another lifetime in the arts. I'd like to plead to the old man, Give me another chance. I still believe in God."

"Do you think about what will happen after you die?"

"I'll be around in some shape or manner. I may be a flash of light, a luminosity. Sometimes, when I watch television, a luminous something comes before my eyes, something comes out of me. I don't know what that is. A light will bulge out of my eyes. Maybe that's the soul, I don't know. We all have souls, there's no doubt about it. Where He is, what He's made of, I don't know. He might be electricity, a force of nature. I know there is something that holds this mystery together. I pray before I start a painting and while I'm working on it. That's why I want another lifetime."

"Do you want another hundred years?"

"Something like that. Maybe fifty, seventy will be enough next time. I'd like to be here again, marry the same woman."

Sometimes in the afternoon Harry and Celia take a nap together, lie together in bed and listen to music, holding hands.

And when the light is good—not too bright and not too dull—Harry sits by the window in his studio and paints. He works with urgency. On some days his hand shakes, one of the many annoyances brought on by his age.

"I'm old," he says.

"What's it like? I ask.

"I don't think I'm enjoying it. I look forward apprehensively. I say to myself, 'Another four or five years, I gotta produce some good painting'—that's what I'm saying to myself. 'Sum it up with some decent painting.' I'll try."

"That would make you happy?"

"That's what makes me happy, yeah. Shapiro was here."

In his whole life, Harry Shapiro has sold one painting, but he never painted for money, anyway.

He's arrived at one hundred in very good physical shape—he's never had a major illness—and researchers at the Albert Einstein College of Medicine in the Bronx are studying him to find out why.

"You know what I think prolongs life?" Harry has said. "Art and music. Beyond that, it is to have a heart full of love. That is the most important thing."

8

SADIE AND
GILBERT HILL

"Sadie can't sleep past six o'clock."

FINDING A hundred-year-old man still married was a surprise to me. But when I met Harry Shapiro in New York, I had been so fixated on his being an artist that I foolishly neglected to ask either him or his wife, Celia, very many questions about their long marriage. Clearly it was part of the reason he was so content. He felt spiritual longing but he was not lonely.

A month later, miraculously, I was given another chance to talk with a married centenarian—two of them, in fact, a husband and wife who live in Florida, both of them one hundred years old. The researchers at the New England Centenarian Study say the odds of a married couple both making it to one hundred are six million to one. Sadie and Gilbert Hill are maddeningly nonchalant about their incredible feat.

"It just kind of caught us standing still," says Gilbert.

"OH MY GOD!" I want to scream. "Married for eighty years!" But I keep quiet and let them talk. Gilbert is chatty. Sadie is not. She just doesn't see the point in going on and on about it.

"The two of you live here alone?" I ask.

"Yup," she says.

"And you do all the cooking together?"

"Yup."

"And shopping and everything?"

"Mmm-hmm . . . yup."

"That's pretty unusual."

"Well, just force of habit, I guess."

"You don't feel like you need any help?"

"Not so far."

Actually, Sadie says, "Not so *fah*."

They are New Englanders—pure Yankee—farmers from birth who scrupulously saved their money and started coming here to central Florida for the winter in 1951. It was mostly agricultural then. They found a quiet town surrounded by orange groves.

"When we come down here, we had just bought a new Mercury car," says Gilbert. "It cost twenty-four hundred and fifty dollars. It was just as good a car as cars today, it just didn't have all the frosting on it."

They made seventy-six one-way trips between Florida and their home near the Vermont-Massachusetts line. And this was before Interstate 95 was built, so they took Highway 301 the whole way. In some places the road hadn't been black-topped.

"One thousand one hundred forty miles," says Gilbert. "We took three days and two nights. Five hundred miles a day was all I wanted to drive at that time," he says, and even after 95 was built, they mostly stayed with 301 anyway, through towns like Sassafras, Maryland, and Pee Dee, South Carolina.

Finally they stopped driving north and south, bought a second car to leave in Florida, and started flying instead. Now they live here year-round.

Sadie and Gilbert Hill were both born in north-central

Vermont, a valley apart. They both lived on dairy farms. Gilbert remembers the first time he saw Sadie, at a dance in Hardwick. It was 1917. He pursued her stubbornly.

"I walked five miles to get to her and walked five miles back home, just to spend two hours with her. I done that several times in the winter."

If he walked, it was a shorter distance than going by road with a team of horses.

"When I used to go and take her to dances, it was ten miles that way. I'd pick her up and take her to the dance, swap teams with my brother, and take her home."

They courted by horse and buggy, and in the winter they would ride in a sleigh, with a blanket and a lantern and heated stones under their feet.

One winter night, after he took Sadie home, Gilbert was riding in the sleigh alone, pulled by a single horse named Prince, when he fell asleep at the reins. Normally, that wouldn't have been a problem since the horse knew the way home. But that night Prince cut a corner while making a turn, one of the sleigh runners hit a stone ledge, and the sleigh tipped over, dumping Gilbert out. He held on to the reins, though, and was dragged up a hill behind Prince in what he calls the gutter, where the horse's hooves had chopped the snow into a slushy mess and all that icy slush went down Gilbert's shirtfront. He gets a good laugh about it. "The horse was all right," he says. "He didn't get near as wet as I did! If I hadn't a-hung on, he'd a-gone home without me!"

(A line from the old Thanksgiving song "Over the River

and Through the Woods" comes to mind: "The horse knows the way to carry the sleigh through white and drifting snow, oh!")

Sadie and Gilbert married in 1920 and were soon hired as farm caretakers for a millionaire landowner. Gilbert worked with the livestock, a herd of more than a hundred registered Jerseys, and part of his job was to take the cattle to livestock fairs around New England. Sadie kept house and cooked, hauling water up and down the stairs, and to make ends meet, they took in boarders, two men who had girl-friends in town. Sadie says she had to keep their white shirts washed and ironed.

In 1929 their landlord lost the farm in the stock market crash, but Sadie and Gilbert had been saving their money and in 1931 they bought their own place. They had two children and continued to work hard. Gilbert remembers that men without work during the Depression took what he calls "make-work jobs" with the Civilian Conservation Corps, "painting trees," he says, going out into the woods to destroy tent caterpillar nests.

During World War II, Gilbert got a job in a defense plant and Sadie and the kids milked twenty cows a day. She says she didn't mind the work. She liked the animals and being outside, too. "It was good while it lasted," she quips.

SADIE AND GILBERT are sitting in side-by-side recliners as we talk, relaxed and attentive, amused, I think, at my questions.

Gilbert is slender and wiry, Sadie is petite and puckish.

His hair is slicked down carefully, hers is short and brushy. They both have thin lips they press together when they smile. And both wear watches with flexible watchbands pushed halfway up their left forearms.

Now and then Gilbert reaches out and takes Sadie's hand in his.

I ask them about their daily routine and Gilbert pipes up enthusiastically.

"We have to get up at six o'clock. Sadie can't sleep after six o'clock. After five, usually. And by six she's raring to get out, get going. If she went all day the way she does in the morning, I don't know where we would end up!" Sadie acknowledges this with the slightest nod.

"She gets out of bed—I timed her this morning, just for fun. I got up first, but while I was in the bathroom, she gets up, she comes out here first and put the coffee on. Got back and washed up and got dressed and just twelve minutes after she got out of bed—*just twelve minutes this morning*—I had her right on the watch."

Sadie chuckles. "I don't have any secrets anymore."

Gilbert goes on. "I timed her. 'T'isn't far from the stove to the breakfast nook, right to the end of the counter."

"So then you have breakfast together?" I ask.

"Oh, yes!"

"And then read the paper?"

"After we get the dishes washed, we sit down and read the paper for a couple of hours."

"What time do you have supper?"

"We have supper at six o'clock. Dinner at twelve, supper

at six, a little something before we go to bed, at eleven o'clock. We used to have coffee then, but the doctor told me it wasn't working good."

"So what do you have now before you go to bed?"

"Orange juice and a cookie. And she has a special drink the doctors give her."

"*En*-sure," Sadie says.

"Do you sleep together?"

"Oh, yes," says Gilbert.

"Do you snore?" I say to Gilbert.

"Not much. She sleeps on her left side ever since I married her, so she don't snore."

I can't bring myself to ask them about sex. They seem modest, especially Sadie. It's not as if I'm in the habit of talking to people about their sex lives, anyway. And in retrospect I'm not sorry I didn't ask. They would have thought it was rude, beyond the bounds of our business here.

The questions I do ask fall into two categories: what their lives were like in the twenties and thirties and what their days are like now.

Back then it was all work; now they socialize. Sadie says, "We have get-togethers and bean suppers. We belong to the Grange and go to that twice a month. We belong to the tourist club, too, that's where we go to dances. And there's the shuffling. . . ."

"Shuffleboard?"

"Oh, yeah, they got a big covered shuffleboard court so they can play in rain or anytime. And we belong to the Methodist Church."

"What kind of dancing do you prefer?"

Gilbert answers. "We do the waltz and the two-step now. We used to do the square dances, but they got a man in that played the organ, and he had a speaker round in front of him and he called the changes right along with the organ. But we couldn't hear. We got to using these things"—he taps his hearing aid—"and they don't work too good, so we quit the squares.

"If I take mine out, I can't hear a thing, not a thing," says Gilbert.

We have a pleasant few hours together. Gilbert gets up only once—to show me a photograph of Sadie when she was young. They are amiable and lighthearted, but they ventured very little that I did not ask about directly. When I told them the interview would be on nationwide radio, I was surprised when Sadie asked me to call her son and daughter to let them know when to hear it. The children's names had not come up in conversation.

Before I left we went outside and they let me take some photographs of them among their roses, and in the hot sun we said our good-byes. They asked me not to mention on the radio what town they lived in because they were starting to get a lot of calls from reporters. I agreed. We stood on the sidewalk making small talk and I realized I was feeling a tug toward them. I didn't want to say good-bye because I knew I would never see them again.

When I got home and tried to write about them for the radio series, Sadie and Gilbert Hill were essentially a mystery to me. They had offered no insight about their longevity and they didn't have anything particularly revealing to say about their long marriage, either.

I listened to the interview over and over, looking for clues, and I kept coming back to the part where Gilbert described their morning routine. ("We have to get up at six o'clock. Sadie can't sleep after six o'clock.") He was so emphatic; it was the most emotion he showed all day.

I called their son in Vermont and I heard Gilbert's voice, twenty-five years younger. Kenneth Hill is retired from the postal service now. Many of his childhood memories are about hard labor.

He says Gilbert was "a bull for work" and "tight as the bark on a maple tree."

"Myself, I'm lazy," he says. "I like to play golf."

He says Sadie and Gilbert don't know how phenomenal their long marriage is. "They just always worked well together. But the first one that dies . . . they can't survive without each other." And did I know, he says, that last year Sadie had cancer?

There had been no mention of that.

I listen to the tape again and now I hear Gilbert's fear of losing Sadie and the fact that she can get their breakfast on the table in "just twelve minutes" is a sign that everything's all right.

I go back to the photographs I took of them among their roses. Gilbert stands straight, his stomach is flat, he has broad shoulders, a high forehead, and a long, thin nose. He looks directly at the camera, without smiling. Sadie is a head shorter, a little hunched over but also trim. Her eyebrows are raised in a bemused way, but she is not smiling, either. They stand side by side, and in the shadow between them, you can see that Gilbert is grasping her arm to steady her, to keep her close. He knows he can't last long without her.

AFTER I VISITED with Sadie and Gilbert, a mild panic began to grow inside me about losing my husband.

My marriage is so short—just fourteen years—compared to Sadie and Gilbert's. How lucky they are to have had so much time together. What can I possibly do to make the years my husband and I have left together mean more?

Each morning that spring I awoke at dawn and lay in bed with the window open, listening for the first mockingbird, hearing the Metro trains coming from Silver Spring. Noah was warm and silent beside me. As I pressed my ear flat against the mattress, I could hear his heartbeat, and its echo.

Be here now, I thought. Be here now.

9

RUTH ELLIS I

"I'm just an ordinary person."

I FOUND RUTH ELLIS in *Ms.* magazine and thought she was beautiful: a slender face, white hair, and dark, smooth skin, both hands held up to her cheeks in a shy gesture. "The oldest living black lesbian in America," the article said. Before long I had her phone number, a file full of newspaper articles about her from around the country, and a film about her life called *Living with Pride: Ruth Ellis @ 100.*

She lives in downtown Detroit in a no-frills apartment building subsidized by the federal government. People say downtown is coming back again, but on this April morning the streets are deserted. There are empty storefronts and greasy-smelling "Coney Island" joints where you can get hot dogs smothered with chili and onions. Look up Michigan Avenue or Grand River or Woodward from here and see stoplights blowing sideways in the wind.

Detroit feels familiar to me. I grew up west of here, twenty miles from Gary, Indiana, where it's also flat, windy, and industrial. We could see the pinkish glow of the blast furnaces on the horizon at night. I thought those tall smokestacks at the steel mill was where clouds were born.

I RING HER bell at the front entrance and Ruth buzzes me into the building. A few men and women are sitting in the fluorescent-lit lobby, just watching to see who comes and goes. In the elevator, a bony young woman with few teeth grins amiably. She has the woozy speech of a drug addict or alcoholic, but her eyes are focused.

"I'm so happy because I've gone back to school," she tells me. "I hope you understand why I am so happy," she says.

The elevator moves slowly between floors. A man on crutches comes and goes silently.

On the thirteenth floor I find Ruth's apartment and knock hard.

"Okay, I'm coming," I hear a voice from inside.

When she opens the door, I'm startled by how tiny she is. Maybe five feet tall, thin, neat, and handsome.

We sit on the love seat in her living room and make small talk. The coffee table holds lots of mail, including newsletters from a group named Golden Threads, a pen-pal club for senior lesbians. She shows me one that includes her profile: "Age 99, Negro, 4'11", 115 pounds, finished high school in Springfield, IL. Like to dance, like bowling and classical music. Mild temperament. Not married. Old fashioned. Do not drink or smoke. Like to receive mail. 'Never too old to Love.'"

I'VE PUT ASIDE the whole week to be with Ruth, finally having gotten it through my head that I need to spend more time with people and let these interviews unfold at their pace and not mine.

It's been arranged that I will drive Ruth to East Lansing, Michigan, today, where she'll speak to students at Michigan

State University. But first we head for the home of her long-time friend Sarah Uhle.

Ruth asks me to put a wheelchair in the trunk of the car, but I find it hard to believe she'll need it. She moves well—with good coordination—though she does complain of stiffness. In the car Ruth is easygoing and open. Her hearing is excellent and her eyesight is, too. She seems confident and in control. She's wearing a gray felt Kangol cap, a man's hat. It gives her a jaunty look.

When we get to Sarah's home in Lansing, I see another side of Ruth. She is childlike and passive in Sarah's presence. They sit on a couch in a near-embrace; Ruth lays her head on Sarah's ample chest.

"Ruth likes her women stout," Sarah laughs.

"She's my prize," Ruth says, closing her eyes.

They met about twenty years ago. Ruth had been happily retired, she says, traveling, for the first time in her life—to California, Niagara Falls, Nassau, Mexico City—with senior-citizen groups. She was in a bowling league, went to dances, played pool, and took yoga classes. She liked being a senior citizen. She says it was the happiest time of her life up until that point.

When Ruth turned eighty, her life changed. A woman named Jaye Spiro, a friend of Sarah's, came to the senior center one day to teach self-defense classes. Ruth liked her immediately.

"I thought she was a lesbian," she says. "She dressed like a lesbian, but I had never met a *white* lesbian. I had no real connection with white people." Ruth sent Jaye a Valentine, asking her if she wanted to get acquainted, and invited her to dinner.

In the film about Ruth, Jaye says she found a kindred spirit in Ruth and asked, "Are you wondering about my lifestyle?" and then went on to tell all her friends about the amazing older woman she had met. Soon Ruth started getting calls from all over the city. Women wanted to take her out for coffee, to go dancing, invite her to dinner. The white lesbian community of Detroit adopted Ruth as their grandmother. They needed a role model. There were so few elder "out" lesbians, and Ruth was lots of fun.

Sarah Uhle was among those women. She has a warm whiskey voice and lustrous, deep, puppy-dog eyes. She is soft and curvaceous next to Ruth's thin angles. Sarah is caring and mothering and Ruth gravitates toward her, reaches out to touch her, snuggles under her arm.

Sarah lives in a comfortable older home in Lansing with two other longtime friends and an old, sweet dog named Smiley. They have an extra room in the back of their house where Ruth stays when she comes to town. It has a bathroom equipped with safety railings and a wide sliding door. Here, Ruth is one of the girls and also an honored elder.

Carolyn Lejuste, one of Sarah's roommates, fusses over Ruth: "You gonna stay overnight with us? Ruth, you want a sandwich? Ruth, are you warm enough? Here, let me turn up the heat for you." The women cater to Ruth, joke with her, get caught up on her news: where she's been, what her plans are.

Ruth tells them she's getting tired. After today, she says, she wants to stop the appearances. Since her hundredth birthday last summer, she's made more than a hundred appearances and now, she says, it's time to stop. In the last year she's been to Washington, D.C., for Gay Pride Day, and to San Francisco for the Dyke March, where she spoke to a crowd of forty thousand. She's been to Toronto and North Carolina and to Provincetown for a Golden Threads gathering. Basically, whatever Ruth wanted to do, her lesbian friends made it happen; they're her personal Make-a-Wish Foundation.

"Yeah, I tell these girls what I want and it happens most of the time," says Ruth.

"Why did all this happen to you, Ruth?" I ask.

"I don't know," she says. "It just fell out of the sky."

But Ruth does know that she is an inspiration to these women, and she knows what kind of effect she has on young people, especially. We head over to the Michigan State University campus in East Lansing for her appointment. It's the day after the Spartans have won the NCAA championship; there's going to be a parade later today at the state capital.

The campus is wide open to a chilling northwest wind. It's a long way from the parking lot to the classroom and Ruth opts for the wheelchair.

We are met in the hallway by Nancy Nystrom, who teaches the class Ruth will address. We can hear Ruth's voice echoing in the classroom behind us as Dr. Nystrom's students watch the film about Ruth's life. Soon, Ruth is wheeled into the room, before a hundred pairs of wide eyes. These are students of social work, mostly undergraduates in their early twenties. They're staring at Ruth. No one says anything. None of them, we learned, has ever met anyone, aside from relatives, more than sixty-five years old.

"Now don't be bashful," Ruth pipes up in a loud voice. "I'm just an ordinary person."

And then a timid voice: "How do you feel about coming out to campuses?"

"I don't mind at all. Maybe you can get inspiration from an old person. A lot of people don't know an old person. You know, we'll be here for quite a while. . . ."

There's laughter all around, including from Ruth. She's read their minds and broken the ice.

A hand goes up. "I would like to know what you would like *us* to know, since we're going to be social workers."

I admire the directness of this question. Ruth sees an opening.

"I would like for the young people to take more interest in some older person. That's what I talk about quite a bit. Now, I know that everybody is busy, the world is going too fast, I think, and you don't have much time for pleasure, but there's a lot of old people that have lost their families, they don't have anyone. There are a lot of lonesome people. And I think if young people would just pick out one person they could go visit, take them to a show or lunch, or something like that . . . Some of them are confined, they don't get to go anyplace, and that gets to be a drag. I had a friend—she lived to be a hundred—and then she decided she was tired. She just stopped eating and she passed."

Ruth pauses to let this sink in and the students are silent.

Then she adds, "I don't want to get that tired. I want to live as long as I can!"

They laugh. This is another Ruth I'm seeing. Strong and upbeat, feeding off their energy.

The questions continue for an hour.

"What would you say to the rest of the world about accepting the gay and lesbian community?"

"I don't see a big difference in our lifestyles. We're human beings just like they are. I don't see what the argument is, why they hate us so."

"Ruth, you've faced so much adversity. What has allowed you to rise above that?"

"I haven't run into much trouble. I've just had an ordinary life. I've had a pretty easy life."

Ruth believes this, but I think what she means is that she doesn't feel that she's been singled out for discrimination. If you engage her on this question, she will admit that blacks and women and lesbians all face difficulties.

"What do you think about sex education in schools?"

"Ooooooooh, honey, you got me there," she declares. She knows they'll laugh at this and she plays it for a moment, shaking her head, but then she gets serious. "I think we deal with sex too early in life. Get your schooling first, then get mixed up with sex. How are you gonna raise children without education? All these children without fathers . . . I don't think they should talk about sex too early. They have all their life to talk about sex."

She pauses for effect here. She knows what's coming next. "Up to age ninety-five, anyway, I can tell you that!" This, of course, brings down the house.

Soon Dr. Nystrom thanks Ruth, gives her an NCAA Champions T-shirt, and invites the students to talk with Ruth privately. "I like to get hugs!" Ruth announces, and they immediately form a line that snakes through the classroom.

Some bend at the waist and she looks up into their young faces, beaming. Some kneel down so she can look directly into their eyes. She listens to each one, asking questions about them, what they're studying, where they are from.

At this moment, engaged, curious, calm, wise, Ruth looks ageless to me, almost young, like someone who wandered into this classroom and just decided to sit in this old wheelchair that someone left behind. She is so small that she puts her feet on top of the footrests, which haven't been flipped down into position. You could not say what decade she was from. She is dignified and demure at the same time.

The young people respond to her openness. She does not lecture them, and finds something to praise in every story she hears. "Oh, you're going too deep now," she says to one. "I can't keep up with that." It's a question about technology.

"What was harder, being a lesbian or a black woman?" a black student asks.

"Being black was harder." Many of the students nod. "People are against blacks. It's not a big deal being a lesbian," she says, "we're just human beings. That's the way I look at things."

"What is the top thing you went through?" one asks. "The highlight of your hundred years?"

"These lesbians and gay people," she says. "When I'm with gay people, I'm happy. They're my family."

I find myself hoping that one day these young people will understand the rarity of Ruth's open mind.

WE'RE IN A cavernous cafeteria in a shopping mall in Lansing called Old Country Buffet where you can find Salisbury steak and fried chicken and mashed potatoes and red Jell-O. All you can eat for a flat price. I feel right at home.

We push together several tables. Sarah and Carolyn, her roommate, and Dr. Nystrom and her partner, plus Ruth and some of Sarah's friends. The women dote on Ruth, carry her plate to the table, bring her a drink, make sure she has the right silverware, and seat her in the middle of the table. They're a fun-loving group, joking about girlfriends past and future, as well as careers and work and politics. They include Ruth in every conversation and she loves the attention.

They are easy to be with, this group of Ruth's friends, who are all over fifty. It doesn't matter to them, or to her, that they are all white and she is black; they love Ruth for who she is, funny and self-deprecating and generous. They love her wisdom and her naïveté. But they love what she represents, too. Her presence is affirming for them.

By the end of the meal, Ruth hasn't eaten much. Her plate is nearly full. Sarah has made sure that all of Ruth's food is soft and easy to chew, but Ruth has just pushed it around on her plate, saying it's hard to swallow.

I am sorry when the dinner is over. Ruth and I drive back to Detroit and we're both tired.

When the elevator door opens onto the thirteenth floor, it's after ten o'clock. As she passes the apartment door next to hers, she raps firmly on it and calls out, "Mary, I'm back!" and keeps moving. She knows her neighbor Mary Parker will come over.

Mary shows up before Ruth has her coat off. Ruth gives Mary a little money every month in exchange for some help around the house. Mary is a sweet-natured lady, probably nearing seventy herself. She has silver hair, in a glamorous pageboy. She has long, slender legs, elegant, manicured nails, and a stylish flair. She also has a chesty smoker's cough. She's known Ruth since she moved into this building thirteen years ago but only recently has come to care for her. Before that, Ruth needed no help. Mary clearly respects and admires Ruth, calling her pet names like "Ruthie" and "Sweetie."

"Mary, please help me. I'm tired. Oh, girl, I'm so tired." Ruth peels her coat off and Mary hangs it up for her. "I'm too tired to do anything. Please help Neenah make that bed."

Ruth has insisted that I stay in her living room for the night and I'm too tired to resist the offer.

Together Mary and I pull a twin bed out from the love seat.

"Will that be okay for you, dear? You sure? Don't you need more blankets?"

I'm so tired I could sleep on the floor.

Ruth comes out of the bedroom and shuffles down the hall toward the bathroom. She has her sweater pulled up around her neck and her slacks pulled down to her knees.

"Oh, I'm so tired. Everything hurts me, Mary."

"Well, let's just get you into bed, Ruth. Did you take your medicine?" Mary leaves me to help Ruth in the bathroom and I take my clothes off and lie down gratefully.

A few hours later I wake up. It must be ninety degrees in the apartment. There's a blast of stale air coming through the vent over my head. I throw the covers off and look out the window toward downtown. The streets are brightly lit.

I can hear Ruth groaning in pain and I'm struck by the unlikeliness of the moment. I am sleeping in the living room of a hundred-year-old person I met this morning. She seemed so lively during the day, but tonight I'm worried she might die. I sleep lightly, aware that Ruth gets up six or seven times during the night. I can hear her in the bathroom.

At daybreak I awaken but she's sleeping. I read in bed until she's moving around. Then she insists on making breakfast for me. Actually, I cook as she stands next to me, telling me what to do. I pour orange juice for both of us, fry two eggs in Wesson oil, slice and fry some Jimmy Dean sausage. Ruth picks up the bottle of oil and pours it over the frying sausage, pressing on the meat with a spatula. She mixes up Aunt Jemima pancake mix and shows me precisely how much to use and exactly where to pour it in the frying pan.

On the kitchen counter I notice Ruth's medications: Vioxx for her arthritis, a potassium supplement, a big bottle of Geritol, which is just vitamins with lots of iron, and a blood-pressure medicine.

I set up some TV tray tables in the living room. Ruth sits in her recliner. She's wearing a pastel plaid wool shirt and white jeans. She looks pretty.

"I sure don't feel pretty," she says as she clicks on the TV with the remote control. The screen fills with a grainy black-and-white shot of the front entrance to the building. She can see who's coming and going.

"I can tell by their walk who it is," she says.

The phone rings.

"Oh, I ain't no good, girl," she tells the caller. "The old gray mare, she ain't what she used to be. Yeah, I'm hurting. I'm hurting all over. My feet, my legs, my arms, my shoulders. I just hurt. Yeah, I've got something to take, but it's not working. It ain't no good, girl. After I come from someplace, I have to recuperate."

Ruth hasn't smiled all morning. She has arthritis in every limb and it's gotten worse in the past year, she says, since she turned one hundred and started doing all this traveling. She holds her body tenderly, as if just the clothes rubbing on her skin hurts. I offer to rub her back and she accepts. I slowly knead the muscles of her shoulders and back. I can feel her ribs. She says, "It feels good when you're rubbing, but it still hurts when you stop."

Ruth is clear about what she wants. "Let's do an interview," she says. "As long as I can lay down, I'm okay." I clip a microphone onto her shirt and she lies down on the love seat. I sit on the floor.

RUTH WAS BORN on July 23, 1899, in Springfield, Illinois, the only girl in her family. She had three brothers and her mother died when she was young. Her father, Charles Ellis, was the first black mail carrier in Springfield.

She says she was "bashful" as a child, didn't want to talk in school.

"I didn't have any friends. I went to school by myself."

"Why, Ruth?" I ask. If I had stopped to think for two seconds I could have figured it out and Ruth knows this. She purses her lips and hums a little tune.

I wait.

"I guess there weren't very many colored in that school," she says finally. "And some of them thought they were better than me. There were a lot of classes where I was the only colored and I was bashful. The teacher would call on me for something and I'd tell her I didn't know. I did know, but I didn't want to stand up before the class."

"Did the kids tease you?"

"No, they didn't pay any attention to me. I was sort of a loner. At lunchtime I'd stand near the schoolyard someplace and watch the rest of the kids play. It wasn't until I got to high school that I had friends, and I didn't accumulate any friends from the white girls. My gym teacher was the only one who paid any attention to me. One teacher slapped me because I was so stupid. I told my daddy the teacher hit me and he came and bawled her out." Ruth's laugh is sad. Her voice turns quiet.

"I didn't get a very good education. If I was to go back to school, I'd have to start from the beginning. That's why I like to be around these young people so much. Maybe I can learn something from them."

I'm stunned by this new view of Ruth, so vulnerable and weak and unhappy as a child. She has managed to turn that hurt into generosity. All her life, she's found ways to give. And now she has taken up the cause of the lonely, outcast elderly, though she doesn't count herself among them.

"Ruth, it's amazing to think that a shy, quiet, lonely little girl is now traveling all over speaking to groups, has a film made about her, and has people saying she's an inspiration to them."

"Yes, it's quite a difference. I guess that's how life works. But I don't ever want to change. I don't want to get uppity. I want to treat people like I want to be treated. I don't want to insult anybody or anything like that. One of the senior cen-ters I go to, people don't pay much attention to one another. They have their cliques. A stranger will come in and they're just there; nobody introduces them. If I see a strange person, I tell them my name. I guess people are sort of cruel. If they don't know you, that's it. A new person comes here in the building, if I don't know them, I try to get to see them."

"Do you think you're like that now because you were so lonely as a little girl? Do you remember that?"

"I don't think about that. I don't think about it. The past, I don't think about much, but I like to be around people. Going around with these college students, maybe some of that can rub off on me. I don't know what they're talking about, but I can listen anyway. Oh, my arm hurts me so."

The phone rings and I bring it to her.

"Oh, girl, the old gray mare ain't what she used to be."

Ruth's phone rings at least twice an hour. Women are calling to see how she is. Every time, she says, "The old gray mare, she ain't what she used to be."

At lunchtime Ruth says she's not hungry, that she's very uncomfortable and wants to go into her room and rest. I ask if I can come back tomorrow. Maybe she'll feel better then.

"That's a good idea," she says.

As I leave the apartment building, I turn to the camera in the foyer and wave.

10

LOUISIANA HINES

"You know, people used to sell people a long time ago."

I STAYED IN Detroit all week and saw Ruth Ellis three more times. To fill the hours between visits, I went for long drives along the river in the rain and listened to deejay Ed Love play jazz on WDET-FM.

One evening I went to visit another centenarian and drove west, out Grand River Avenue, which cuts through one struggling commercial district after another: liquor stores and Coney Island restaurants and vacant lots and plastic bags flattened against chain-link fences by the wind.

The woman I wanted to meet has the musical name of Louisiana Hines, and I knew very little about her except that her grandfather was a slave.

She lives in a brick Tudor-style home on a side street off Grand River. There are white cement planters full of red plastic roses on either side of the front steps.

Her granddaughter, Darlene House, meets me at the door. As she takes my coat, I see a woman out of the corner of my eye, in the living room, shoving furniture into place and plumping pillows. I assume that Mrs. Hines has live-in help, but Darlene calls the woman over and says, "This is my grandmother, Louisiana."

She shakes my hand firmly. Her hands are large and strong but she is shy. She is wearing a floral-print dress (of her own design, she tells me later) and black basketball shoes.

She looks and acts far younger than any centenarian I have met, even Anna Wilmot.

She chooses a velvet armchair to sit in and I perch on the edge of the couch, next to her. She bounces around in the chair like a child, smoothing out her skirt, leaning forward and back. She seems nervous, which is a surprise to me. I respond by trying to be ultra-cool and laid-back, to put her at ease before we start. This is one of my better acts. Actually I'm nervous, too. She smiles politely and nods a lot, but as I clip the microphone on, I know it's a little too soon.

She was born in Luverne, Alabama—"out from Green-ville"—in 1899, to Ben and Callie Summerlin.

Her mother had eleven children, "but she only raised seven. Some of them I never see. People didn't tell you what they was expecting. You don't know what happened. It wasn't your business. They didn't tell you about their private self."

Her father was a farmer.

"He raised peanuts and cane and had a big garden. They was lucky about using the *Ladies Birthday Almanac*. There was a time to plant his cane, a time for peanuts. They went by the almanac."

Louisiana remembers they always had lots of food. Her father kept hogs and cows and her mother was always busy in the kitchen. "They called her Cookin' Callie," she says proudly.

I jump right to what I'm most curious about: "Were your parents born into slavery?"

"No, my grandparents were. But their master was a good man, Jack Bimbo. No whippin', no, no. Nobody whoop his

Negroes. Anybody put the hand on his Negroes, he said, he put the gun on them. And he let them dance all night."

"Do you know where your parents were from?" I ask.

"You know, people used to sell people a long time ago. You never know where your mama or your daddy was from, all like that. They told me about that. My mother carried me down the road to the plantation where my granddaddy used to work. The house was gone. But the land where he used to work was there."

"What did she tell you?"

"Well, she said that was the place where her daddy said he worked. He worked there and Bimbo lived there."

As she tells me these things, I sense that Mrs. Hines isn't getting any more comfortable and so my own nervous response is to change the subject, instead of pressing on. I ask about her childhood, more about her mother and her grand-parents and finally, how she came to be married to Arthur Hines. She met him in church, she says. Her family were "church people."

"People didn't court like they do now. They weren't on your lap and on your neck. When that boy come in, he couldn't come too soon and he couldn't stay too late." She laughs a high, giggly laugh. "He come between two and three o'clock. He could stay there till the clock struck nine. When it struck eight-thirty, you got thirty minutes to stand on your feet and reach for your hat, that's right, and be gone. And you ain't been in his lap, you ain't been on his neck. You get the hat and you hand it to him and he takes his hat and when he starts down the steps he put his hat on."

"Things were very formal," I note.

"Very strict. Not only for me, but for the other girls around, too. The boys come to see you and not to hold you. We thought we was having a nice time, sitting there with our starched dresses on." She smiles.

"Who talked to you about sex before you got married?"

"Nobody. Ain't nobody told me nothing. The way that was, it's kinda funny, I thought when a boy come to see you a good while, it's time to get married. Four years he came. Every other Sunday. Yeah. That's right!"

"He must have really wanted to marry you."

"No. Oh, I don't know. You see, the boys didn't have much more sense than we had." She laughs again. "Lord, have mercy. That was a long time ago. It's just pitiful the things that you know now that they didn't know then. People didn't talk to you and tell you things."

I want to know about being black in the South at the turn of the century and she is obliging. She tells me about her doctor, a white man who she says was "one of the best doctors that ever put on a pair of pants." After a while I won-der if she isn't going out of her way to mention only good things that had happened between the races in Alabama.

"Did you hear about lynchings when you were growing up, or activities of the Klan?" I ask.

"Oh, my Lord, yes. They would do that. There's good ones and mean ones. You didn't have to do nothin'. If they got a chance to beat you up, they would."

"Did you know people who were lynched?"

"Not far from us lived Mama's cousin George Teague. He

was a preacher. He was preaching all about the Bible, that all men are created equal. Some people don't believe it. The white people in the Southern states, they didn't think we were created equal to them no kinda way. No way. 'Don't be sayin' that. Not *equal*.'

"Well, some men had gone and told the white people, 'He's telling us we're equal with you white people,' and the whites said to him, 'You better not be preaching that all men's created equal.' They said, 'He cannot be equaling you Negroes with us.' He said, 'I'm preaching what the Bible says and I can't stop preaching what the Bible says.' Well, they overheard him sure enough. And they came and got him and they killed him.

"They took him and drug him all over the place. He had two or three little boys, and they said if they didn't kill them, they'd be just like George Teague, and they killed the little boys, too. *Small* boys. *Little* boys. They might have throwed them in the Blue Creek. And he also had a little girl named Rosie. A white lady said, 'Don't kill her, she's a pretty little girl.' She's the prettiest little black girl they ever looked at. She had beautiful eyes. And the white ladies begged them not to kill her."

The girl was spared.

Mrs. Hines's story veers off into a bit of preaching about how Jesus didn't have a front door and a back door on the church and soon, as these things go, she's telling me about how she and her husband came to Detroit and how much she enjoyed her work in an airplane factory during World War II. She was a riveter, a real Rosie the Riveter.

But it's late, I'm tired and not following up questions very sincerely. We've talked for two hours and I can't go on. I've had too much input, there are too many images floating in my head. I ask to stop. Louisiana Hines is gracious and she seems relieved.

11

RUTH ELLIS II

"They just want to know me
'cause I'm a hundred."

THE NEXT MORNING I have some free time. Ruth is expecting me in the afternoon. I take the chance to read and write and think at the downtown Starbucks. Outside the tall windows a man and woman have arranged rows of white plastic buckets full of flowers for sale. They both look a little hungover, in jeans and denim jackets. The man has straggly blond hair and a cigarette dangling from his lip. He lifts the yard-high bouquets of dyed carnations, shakes them, and rolls them in white paper. On my side of the window, the men and women are dressed for business in suits and sports coats, leather-soled shoes, and designer eyewear. I feel separate from both worlds, the one outside on the street and the one here inside, but glad to be warm and alone. If I smoked, I would. I write down everything I can remember about my last few days in Detroit visiting Ruth.

A number of times Ruth has said, "I wasn't really aware of my life until I was eighty." I think she meant that she didn't think of herself as anything special until all the younger women started looking up to her. We are very different, Ruth and I.

As a child I was told that I *was* special and smart and could do whatever I wanted to do. I was a good student, a good athlete. I always got chosen to be on teams. I took dancing lessons and piano lessons and was the drum major of my high-school marching band. But Ruth was told she was stupid, and maybe she didn't completely believe it, but it made her hang back. She was alone and lonely as a child. Her mother was dead. It was her brother who showed her how to make clothes for her doll. And she didn't go to college like her brothers. It wasn't an option.

Once she moved to Detroit, she had a companion for many years, a younger woman named Babe, who was outgoing and party-loving and cheated on Ruth. But they opened their home to black gay men and women who could not socialize in public. They had parties with music and dancing and card playing and drinking and sometimes fighting. Ruth and Babe gave people a place to live when they needed it, folks who had just arrived in Detroit from the South. They even helped some get through college. Ruth gave other people what she never had.

I've spent a lot of time furthering my career, myself, and following some vague notions about truth. I've spent a lot of time trying to be smart instead of trying to do good, admiring "smart" people instead of good people.

When I see how Ruth touches people—those young college students in Lansing, for example—when it's such a huge physical effort for her, I realize I have a long way to go.

BACK AT HER apartment a few blocks and a whole world away from Starbucks, I ask Ruth if she wants to go for a drive. It's windy and cold again, but she hasn't been outside since we went to Lansing three days ago. I suggest that we drive by the new baseball park and she's up for that. Soon we're walking through the lobby on the way to the car. Everyone there knows Ruth.

"Hello, Miss Ellis," they say.

These are the people Ruth referred to in Lansing—older people who have no family, who could benefit from the attention of some younger person who could take them to a show, as she said, or out to lunch. The people sitting here have no place to go. They're waiting for some friendly company to chance by and Ruth is it. She stops and chats. Mary Parker told me that until recently, Ruth did the grocery shopping for many of these older residents of the building who can't get out anymore, all of them younger than she is.

We drive the few blocks to Comerica Field, the new home of the Detroit Tigers, which is set to open to the public the next day. I ignore the parking barricades in order to get Ruth as close as possible so she can see the huge tiger sculptures, the baseballs and bats incorporated into the design, the ticket windows. We slowly drive the streets on all four sides. Ruth approves and tells me she saw Satchel Paige pitch once at the old Tiger stadium.

Just south of Comerica Field is a drugstore called Paul's. Ruth gives me a few dollars and sends me in to get something for her. I run across the street and find myself in a place that carries products that I am mostly not familiar with. An entire wall is devoted to hair products, mostly straighteners and relaxers. The pharmacist directs me to what I've come for, Sloan's Liniment. The label says to apply it with cotton balls.

In the checkout line, the woman in front of me is buying snuff. Behind the cashier are lined up ten different kinds of it.

"Ruth, I've never seen snuff for sale," I tell her as I give her the liniment in the car.

"Girl, they've got everything you might need in there."

We spend the afternoon driving slowly around downtown Detroit, Ruth telling me stories about places she remembers. She knows exactly where we are at all times. We go out to Belle Isle, an island in the Detroit River, north of downtown. It's a park full of green, open space, marinas, and coves where swans are dawdling. There's a small lighthouse on the north end. Again I ignore the signs and drive across a field to a grassy point, thinking Ruth might like to be surrounded by the natural world for a moment without having to get out of the car. Ruth remembers coming here for summer concerts, sleeping on the grass under the stars because it was so hot in town.

We drive to the southern tip of the island as it begins to rain. We can see downtown just a few miles away, dwarfed by the sky and the water, both gray and angry. There is no hint of spring in the wind.

"Let's go to Big Boy," Ruth chirps.

I'm marveling a little bit that Ruth has agreed to drive around with me like this. I'm practically a stranger to her. Inside the brightly lit restaurant a young man comes to wait on us.

"Do you know how old I am?" Ruth smiles.

"Well, no, I don't." He smiles broadly. He's onto her.

"I am one hundred years old!"

"No! You can't be! Well, honey, you look just great!"

"Thank you. I'll have a bowl of vegetable beef soup."

"Yes, *ma'am,*" he laughs.

Ruth eats very slowly, picking out the cubed vegetables and the strands of beef one by one. As she eats, people come by.

"I just wanted to say hello and give you a hug," says a young waitress.

Ruth gives hugs. I'm guessing she comes here often.

"Ruth, do you know all these people?" I ask.

"No, honey," she says. "They just want to know me 'cause I'm a hundred."

I SPENT MORE time with Ruth Ellis than I had with any other centenarian. She took me into her life, her home, and her circle of friends without hesitation. She had no pretenses, nothing to hide. I saw her in many moods: strong and funny in front of the students, groaning in pain at four A.M., confidently pouring cooking oil on my breakfast sausage, and now, at the end of my visit, it seems that I have known her longer than five days.

As I stand in her living room with my coat zipped up to my chin, ready to drive to the airport, she says, "You know, I never did understand the difference between jet planes and propellers," so instead of delivering an elaborate good-bye, I try to explain what I know about jet propulsion. It seemed fitting at the time.

As my jet climbed eastward toward home, I could see downtown Detroit. I searched Ruth's neighborhood for her apartment building and Comerica Field and then I found Belle Isle, too, and the Big Boy restaurant, all the places we had been together—for the first time and the last.

12

ROY LARKIN STAMPER I

"I need a companion, real bad."

I'M DRIVING EAST from Tulsa, Oklahoma, on the Cherokee
Turnpike, listening to Reba McEntire on the radio. It's late
May and the fields are lush. The tall grasses come right up to
the edge of U.S. Highway 412, and from the crest of a hill, the
countryside feels timeless.

I turn onto a two-lane road, the scenic route to the town
of Locust Grove, and pass a roadhouse, a taxidermy shop, and
a church called the Lighthouse, "Where Jesus Is Real." The
road curves left and I can see a Sinclair gas station and a faded
yellow stoplight swinging overhead.

Locust Grove is a few long blocks from end to end.
There's a convenience store, a restaurant, a Laundromat, and
on the far end, another convenience store: Greg's Git 'n Split.
I turn toward the highway, a new Holiday Inn Express, and
see Greg's other competitor, the "Git 'n Go."

I'm here to visit 103-year-old R. L. Stamper at the
Stamper Quarter Horse Ranch. I call up Claude Stamper,
R. L.'s son. As has been the case the other times I've called,
he's in his truck when he answers.

"You wanna come by tonight?" he offers. But I decline,
thinking I'll go to bed early. He gives me directions to the
ranch for tomorrow. I'm about fifteen minutes away.

But I'm restless and the mattress is rock hard and the
room is so new that everything smells of chemicals, so I

decide to drive by the ranch and scope it out. I stop in town to buy a local paper, then drive toward the ranch. I pass very few cars on the narrow roads and the mailboxes are far apart. I head north, the setting sun on my left, and cross a wide river meandering through the countryside.

I drive until dusk and never find the ranch, so I cross many sets of parallel railroad tracks and turn south again, passing a huge industrial site rising out of green fields, no sign identifying it. It's many stories tall, with a high chain-link fence all around. It's well-lighted, but not a soul is visible. I can't tell what it is and I think of Karen Silkwood. No one knows where I am but me.

Back at the hotel, I let CNN blast at me until well after I fall asleep. I get up at 2:12 to shut it off and sleep with a vague dread.

THE NEXT MORNING is gloriously clear and fresh. I find the Stamper Quarter Horse Ranch easily this time and pull over onto the grassy shoulder to see it spread along the south side of the road. Green fields are sprinkled with reddish horses and colts and the land sweeps away toward wooded hills a mile back. There's a barn, a long horse trailer, and a cluster of low buildings under trees. I can make out two houses from here. A hot west wind comes over the treetops, turning the leaves over until their pale undersides flash and ripple.

WHEN I WAS growing up, my brother and I were outdoor kids. We lived in the woods near the Little Calumet River, just a couple miles south of Lake Michigan in northern Indiana.

Our parents were from Chicago, born on the South Side, the children of Croatian immigrants. When they got married in 1950, they couldn't wait to get out of the city. They bought land and built a house. My mother was always chasing us out to "get fresh air."

My brother, Leigh, was a serious fisherman before he was ten years old, and I liked to go along and play with the worms and bobbers. He had a BB gun and I had a knife. We rode our bikes everywhere—through grassy fields, on gravel roads, and through the mud. In winter we skated on the thin river ice and sledded with devotion. We had a treehouse enclosed with screens all around and a trapdoor to the roof.

We had dogs, of course, and we brought home baby rabbits, snapping turtles, snakes, tadpoles, butterflies, and lightning bugs we kept in jars. We had countless baby chicks and ducklings we got at the feed stores that never made it to adulthood: They'd escape or get killed by weasels. I was sure that one day I would have a raccoon.

Our house was on a clifftop with a long, open view of the woods and swampy riverbottom. I always imagined I could see Indians out there, running on our paths, jumping over logs, plants slapping their legs. We knew about the Chippewa who had lived here before us—just a few years before us, I thought—and I half-expected to come upon a Chippewa campfire. To me, they were superhuman: strong and brave and silent. They knew how to live in the woods, what to eat, how to make everything they needed.

As young Hoosiers, we learned in school that our state

had been the frontier just a hundred years before and we knew that Abraham Lincoln was ours, raised in Indiana in a log cabin, learning to read by firelight. As a child, I could respect that. I think it's part of why I fell so hard for 103-year-old Roy Larkin Stamper.

A LONG, TREE-LINED lane welcomes me to the Stamper ranch. There's a pickup in the driveway of the first house I come to, and close by, a sun-bleached seventies Cadillac is slumped in front of another house. I figure the first vehicle belongs to Claude, the second to his father, R. L.

Claude Stamper talks in a soft, sweet voice. His eyes are black, he's tanned and looks strong, though he limps. He quickly brings out a scrapbook to tell me about the family. His son DeWayne runs the quarter-horse business, and his other sons live nearby. Claude has a house-moving business now; it keeps him driving the hundred-mile round-trip daily from Tulsa, which would seem to be why I always reach him by cell phone in his truck.

He tries to give me coffee and breakfast, opens the freezer door to show me a pile of frozen sausage biscuits in cellophane wrappers. "Just need to throw one in the microwave," he says. "Daddy likes these. I make breakfast for him sometimes." Claude lives alone in this house. His wife died last year.

We walk across the driveway and up a wooden ramp to the house next door. We pass through a large living room with shag carpeting and brocade furniture. There's a spinet piano along one wall and a grandfather clock taller than I am against another. In the kitchen there's dark paneling, some dishes drying on a rack, a bottle of blue Aqua Velva after-shave on the counter. In a small room off the kitchen sits a thin, pale man wearing a cowboy hat and seated on a motor-ized scooter, facing us.

"Daddy, this is the lady I told you about who's come to interview you."

Roy Larkin Stamper flashes a toothy, gold, sparkly smile.

"Well, aren't you nice to come all this way to see me?"

His face is moist and pink from just having shaved. He's wearing a plaid shirt, polyester pants, and orange ostrich cowboy boots that look as if they're right out of the box.

He sweet-talks me.

"Well, aren't you the prettiest little thing?"

I grin.

Claude leaves us and I suggest that we do the interview in the living room.

R. L. motors into the room on his three-wheeled scooter and turns the swivel seat to face me. I reach up and clip the microphone onto his shirt. His breath is sweet.

"How's your hearing, Mr. Stamper?"

"Pretty good," he says.

"How's your vision?"

"Well, not so good." He's leaning down and toward me. His blue eyes are clear and focused.

"I need to get a level on your voice," I begin. "What did you have for breakfast?"

"I had a sausage biscuit and some oatmeal."

"What can I call you?"

"I go by R. L. My name's Roy Larkin but most everybody calls me R. L."

And very soon we are far away in time and place.

"I was raised in the eastern part of Kentucky. Lee County, Wolfe County, and Powell County. That's where the feud was," he says, referring to the infamous Hatfield and McCoy dispute of the late 1800's.

My husband's family is from Kentucky but not the eastern part. That's the notorious mountain region where the isolation and the Scots-Irish clannishness of the settlers combined to create a culture that many outsiders believe is still dangerous.

When R. L. was growing up, it *was* violent. He was born in 1896.

"The times were real rough," he says. "We lived hand-to-mouth. And there was lots of killin' and murderin' and feudin' all the time. But you know, them robbers was good, moral men. They didn't rob the poor, I remember. And my daddy, he wouldn't know how to lie. He was a good, honest man. He got into some trouble, however."

"The trouble" was what R. L. calls "shootin' scrapes." His daddy lent a gun to a man who didn't want to return it, he says, and they dueled over it in front of the Stamper cabin one day. His father beat the man to the draw and "shot him twice about the heart." The man fell in the yard, "mort'ly wounded."

They put R. L.'s father under house arrest, so he made a plan to leave, to go west. He came to R. L. one night and asked if he wanted to go with him to Indian Territory.

We are less than half an hour into our interview and I am already completely sucked in, my mind reeling. R. L. is just warming up, smiling and laughing. I'm sure my eyes must have been wide, and no doubt that fed his fire.

"Did you go to school in Kentucky, R. L.?"

"Oh, I guess for about a week. We lived in a place called Hall Holler and I had to walk three mile. My lunch was a piece of cornbread. We set on split logs. They built a new school and called it Omega. I went there a little while and got up to the fourth grade. But I got ashamed because I got big, so I quit. I couldn't write and couldn't read."

"When your daddy decided to go west, why did he bring you?"

"He just hated to leave me, I guess. Him and me was real partners. I'd hold his pant leg on the wagon. I was a pretty good-size kid, nine years old."

R. L.'s father had twenty-one children to care for. He had been married twice before marrying R. L.'s mother, and she brought two kids to the marriage. R. L. was among the youngest.

"I trusted him. He was the Lord to me and he was really good to me. My other brothers and him didn't get along. They was more of a criminal element than I was. They fought and killed till they died."

R. L. and his father went to Lexington, Kentucky, and caught a train, heading for what is now Tulsa. There they switched to a freight train going toward Dawson, where his father had a brother.

"He told me there was a grade just outside Dawson and the train might slow up for that. Well, we musta went over the grade and the train's a-flyin' and he was gonna show me how to get down off the train. He stepped down there off the train, just end over appetite, and just rolled down through there with dust a-flyin'!"

R. L. is grinning. He knows it's a great story.

"And I clumb down the step, just about four feet to the ground, and the first place I hit, the top of my head! And I rolled down—I was just a kid, you see? Now, wasn't that a deal?"

Yes, I admit that it was.

"And then he left me there, with his brother, till he got located, and then he brought me to Choteau and left me at a hotel for a week."

His father left a nine-year-old child at a hotel alone for a week while he went on horseback from Choteau to Locust Grove, ten miles away, and made a deal for some land.

R. L.'s father bought the land we are sitting on, nearly one hundred years ago. The very acres I saw this morning, he must have seen from the same high spot where I parked my car. He would have been on horseback with a land broker who would have pointed south and said, "It goes up into those hills there, back to the river. . . ." And they would've talked of water and timber and markets and how to clear the hilly, rocky land. Mr. Stamper paid ten dollars an acre. It would need a lot of hands to make it pay.

The next spring, in 1906, the rest of the family came out from Kentucky.

I ask R. L., "When you first came here, what was it like? Who lived in this country?"

"No*body*. Nobody but the Indians. There wasn't a white man in the country. I had to learn to talk Cherokee before I could spark." He means go courting.

Stamper speaks a line of Cherokee and grins widely.

I fall for this. "What does that mean?"

"You sure enough are a pretty girl!"

We both laugh.

"How did the Indians live at that time?" I ask.

"They just lived off the land. And they had a stomp ground a mile from here where they'd dance around. There was an ash hopper where they kept a fire that never went out. It was there for years. And they would dance around it till midnight. They had a pole and they'd dance."

He sings a few lines for me in Cherokee.

"They might have been celebrating burning a white man, I don't know!"

"You went to see that?"

"Oh, I went to that regular, yeah, once a month or so. I got along good with the Indians. They treated me real good. And I was good to them. I never did have no run-ins with them."

The Stamper family cleared their ranch land and did a little bit of everything to survive. They planted peaches and apples and strawberries for cash. They got some cows for milk and R. L.'s mother made butter. They'd hang the milk in the well or in the spring to keep it cool.

"We raised a little cotton, not too much. We'd pick cotton and take it and buy groceries. In the fall, we'd kill hogs, render the meat out, and the lard would last over the winter.

It was fat with a lot of salt. We'd eat that. Now it would kill you, I guess. We worked all the time. *All* the time. Work me to death."

"You did everything yourselves."

"I don't know how. I don't know how in the world Daddy ever took care of us. That's been a mystery to me. We used a sled and oxen called Buck and Darb. The sled had runners. They'd wear this sled out, the runners, then get another timber, take the bark off—I guess it was a willow or something. We didn't see a wagon till later."

WE'VE BEEN TALKING a couple of hours by now and R. L. Stamper is still right in front of my face, the rim of his cowboy hat nearly touching my forehead. I can smell his Aqua Velva. It's getting warm in the room and I'm riveted by these stories. He's not slowing down, but he is starting to ramble. I have to keep bringing him back to the family story, even though the digressions are fascinating, too.

"Do you remember the dust storms and the Depression in the thirties?" I ask.

"That storm was awful. We tied blankets over the windows. In Kansas it was real bad, it was worse than here. But many people just packed up and left. Some went to California if they could."

The government brought flour and fruit to the Stamper ranch. They had a garage, R. L. says, where the food could be stored for distribution to the neighbors.

"They come here with apples and oranges and all kind of

fruit, and my children stood and watched and their mouths watered, but we have never taken a dime of relief. No way."

It was during this time that a number of outlaws were making names for themselves, including Pretty Boy Floyd and Bonnie and Clyde. Stamper remembers Floyd especially.

"They come here, located right here in this community. They'd come over here on horseback." He points south toward the cliffs on his land and says someone stashed their loot up there in a cave. "But they was good fellows," he insists, "they's just robbers." He understands their motivation. People were desperate, he says. "One night I looked at my little wife and my little girl—she was six years old. They didn't have a coat. No sweater. And I couldn't take that. I said, 'Honey, I'm leaving here tonight.' I caught a freight train and when I got off I didn't have anything. I was cold. I told that boss, 'I want to go to work. I got a wife and a little girl and I'm broke. I got to work.' And I went to work in a coal mine. I had a light on the bill of my cap and there were little mules down there. I stayed there that winter. Well, I got this little girl a red coat and for my wife a big plaid sweater, and I paid the grocery bill. I come home and they was having a revival. And I got to thinking about the Lord and the future. I just decided to straighten out, quit drinking, quit carousing, quit moonshining."

And R. L. Stamper started preaching.

"I guess I was about thirty-two. I was praying here under a walnut tree. I had a bunch of chickens, my horses, cattle, and home, and something said, 'Can you leave all that, everything, and go with me?' And I said, 'Yeah.' The Lord just impressed me, not with an audible voice. 'I want you to go and preach.' I couldn't read and write. It was hard to say I would, but I said I would and the thought come, 'When?' And I said, 'Wednesday night.' I went to the schoolhouse and I preached on Revelation. I didn't know any more than a hog knows a sidesaddle, but God honored it. He just done it. I just furnished the men and He furnished the grace."

Looking back on those first few hours of talking about his life, I realize that Stamper had been talking about the Lord since we started, but I was not focused on it. I was more interested in hearing about pioneer life in Oklahoma. I've met plenty of preachers, and people who've been saved, but none who could describe what was essentially a frontier existence. I was amazed at what he and his family went through, and I wonder if I could endure a life like that. As he recounted the stories, he seemed amazed, too, and credited God with his survival.

At some point he decides to really lay into me. Maybe he thinks that I am not sufficiently impressed with his relation-ship with the Lord. I ask him a vague, sweeping question: "A child born today, will he see the kinds of changes you've seen?"

"No, and I'll tell you why. We're at the *end* time. Our land is wore out, the population increases, water is contami-nated, all the food, your grass, and everything. And *right now,* I'm a-talkin' to *you,* who's hearing some of the last words of this age. *You may not get back to Tulsa.* The Lord is coming without a doubt. He said, 'I will be back' . . . but I'm getting off the subject."

He leans back in his scooter and pauses, dramatically, I think, waiting for me to respond.

Well. I can feel the hair on the back of my neck standing

up and that surprises me. He leans forward. "We're at the *end* time and the next message I preach, it may be the last. That's not to say He's coming tonight or tomorrow, but I say He could."

"So you don't think the world is gonna last another hundred years?" I say.

"Oh, no! I don't think it's gonna last another *year*. I didn't think I'd see another birthday. No, no. It *can't*."

"But people have been saying that for a long time and it hasn't happened."

He's revved up, talking fast.

"Jesus said . . . well, maybe you want to hear something else. . . ."

But he goes on with something about matrimony and the days of Noah that I don't quite follow.

R. L. HAS BEEN preaching for about seventy years now. In the thirties, he traveled the region, preaching wherever he could, mostly in rural communities, like the one he's from. And he says he often got in trouble for it, got beat up because some people didn't like him preaching what's known as "holi-ness," meaning conservative, moralistic lessons. He tells me over and over that he never took any money for preaching, always gave the collection back, often to a parishioner going through hard times. He takes long detours into what I call "What the Bible Says About That" stories that mostly don't engage me, but instead give me long stretches of time to think about him or watch him. So this moment when my hair stands on end surprises me. I don't believe the end of the world is coming, but he does, and I can feel the fire that's burning him up. He wants to save souls. He wants to save me. But more important, he wants to get out in the world and, as he says, be a fisherman for souls. But he can't. He's stuck here on the ranch. He has family around—his son and his grandson and his daughter and many grandchildren all live nearby—but he's lonely for work. And he has no wife to look after him and help him. His third wife died last year.

"My little wife, she was Indian. She was one of the best women that ever lived in the world. Real sweet lady. She spoilt me. A real dandy. She waited on me like I was a baby. And when she died, they carried a hundred and fifty dresses out of here. That's the kind of husband I am."

And then comes the big pitch.

"I need a companion, real bad. But I don't mix and I don't see nobody and the one I'd have probably wouldn't have me. What would a woman want with an old man?"

He answers his own question.

"I've got income I could give a woman. Fifty dollars a day. I've got property. I've got a Cadillac worth fifteen, twenty thousand dollars. I've got a home. I've got a lot to offer a woman yet, but I sit here, and it's real boresome. If you didn't have the Lord, you'd crack up."

He means this. He's thought it out.

"I can preach from a wheelchair and I don't have to have the Bible. I couldn't take a woman my age, I'd have to have a younger woman. It would have to be a miracle from God. Somebody who'd have a missionary spirit and a love for the Lord to come and drive me. Because if I'm able to talk to you, I'm able to preach. The Bible said, 'When you're old you can still bear fruit and be fat and flourishing.' Well, I like that. That's me."

This talk of a new wife seems outlandish to me. He's 103 years old. But he is not kidding. He says he has a burden for lost souls.

We've been talking for four hours and I'm exhausted. He is still right in front of my face and he says he could keep going, but I can't listen anymore. I've got to go and think about all this.

I return to my hotel and lie down on the cool, slick bedspread as if steam were rising from my body. That night, in my journal I write, "Roy Larkin Stamper is a wild man, a little frightening."

I'd had that falling feeling again and this time it was stronger.

I GO BACK the next day and spend a few hours in the horse barn with R. L.'s grandson DeWayne, who runs the horse business now. The Stampers are famous for their cutting horses, specially trained to "cut" individual cattle from a herd. It's a big sport in this part of the country. People travel far to attend competitions for thousands of dollars in cash prizes. People come here to have DeWayne Stamper train their horses and to buy horses from him. He is tall and soft-spoken and polite. He's wearing cowboy boots and spurs, chaps and a cowboy hat. Hanging from his belt is a cell phone.

He lets me look around the horse barn and the indoor arena, then we call over to the house to find R. L. He seems hurt that I didn't come and see him first. He wants to be part of the action. I go to the house and get him. He's sitting in a motorized wheelchair instead of his three-wheeled scooter, and he buzzes across the gravel driveway toward the barn, followed closely by a Border collie that wants him to stop and throw a tennis ball. He does.

At the barn he brags about DeWayne elaborately, calls him "bulletproof in every way" and "tops in his business," and asks him to show me Sweeping Cow, their current champion cutting horse. Cutting horses are new to me, but I can tell Sweeping Cow is well cared for, muscular and alert.

We drink Mountain Dews in the barn office and then R. L. and I head back to the house, stopping in the grass to catch a breeze from across an open field to the west. It's a hot, clear morning and R. L. is suddenly wistful. He says he really doesn't care much about the horse business anymore. Says the kids don't really appreciate what he's done for them, how much he's given them, and he says the horses aren't tough like they used to be. One winter night eighty years ago, he says, he rode a horse all night to Pryor—about thirty miles away—just to go "sparkin'." He says he about froze his ears, but "the horse loped every step of the way." A horse couldn't do that today, he says, they're too soft and pampered from living in barns. He stops short of saying that about the people around him, too. Both Claude and DeWayne seem respectful and proud of R. L., what he's done for them and what he's accomplished. But what the power dynamics of this family are, I have no idea. I do know that a family business is a complicated thing.

We go back to the house and spend a few more hours talking, mostly about the end of the world, which doesn't scare me the way it did yesterday. Now I realize it's a theme R. L. has playing in his head over and over. And today he's not sitting close to my face, staring into my eyes. The spell is broken.

We're in his den, a long, masculine room with a fireplace and a wall that's covered floor to ceiling with brass horse trophies, glinting in the late afternoon light like individual flames. It's impressive and I take some pictures of him there. He looks solemnly toward the camera, but he can't see exactly where the lens is, so his gaze is a little off. Suddenly he reaches up and takes a small statuette off a shelf, a brass pony on a pedestal. The plaque says 1959. TOPEKA HORSE SHOW.

He thrusts it into my hands.

"Here, I want you to have this," he says.

He's not playful and funny today. He seems distracted and tired and lonely. I accept his gift as a farewell, and soon I say, "Well, I think I'll be leaving now," and he doesn't protest but says he wants to pray for me.

R. L.'s hands are crooked and scarred from 103 years of working with shovels and hammers and barbed wire. He crumples them together, closes his eyes, and prays out loud: "Lord, protect her as she drives her little car back to Tulsa."

Just as I did yesterday, I feel a cool breeze on my neck and I know again the depth of his belief.

As I head down the driveway and onto the blacktopped road, I recall R. L. telling me that he remembers when there was just one fence between here and Tulsa. Now I have seen this land through his eyes—as it was a hundred years ago, in its wild state—and I'm sad now, as he is, about the changes.

THERE WAS A time in my life when I might have agreed to drive R. L. around the countryside in his old Cadillac so he could save souls at revivals. Twenty-five years ago I had just graduated from college and spent the summer at the Minnesota Outward Bound School in the Boundary Waters Canoe Area. For a month we lived in the wilderness, cooking over fires, sleeping through thunderstorms, carrying canvas packs and aluminum canoes in swampy muck up to our thighs, rappeling down cliffs. When that month was over, I was strong and fearless. I cut off my hair with a pair of borrowed scissors and drove my Toyota west, across the Dakotas, Wyoming, Montana, Oregon, and Washington, following the trail of Lewis and Clark to the Pacific. I went to Vancouver Island, down to San Francisco, and then to Yosemite, Death Valley, the Grand Canyon, and back across the Rockies and Kansas and home to Indiana. If, on that trip, I had found myself in Locust Grove at the Stamper ranch and R. L. had been looking for someone to drive him around, I might have done it. I had nothing to lose at twenty-two, and, even then, I think I would have known that men like R. L. Stamper would soon be gone from this world.

13

HELEN BOARDMAN

"I guess I'm an optimist."

MY EDITOR AT NPR, Neva Grant, thought I'd fallen in love with R. L. Stamper.

"If I didn't know you were happily married, I'd say you were seduced," she said.

"It wasn't love, Neva," I said, though I had fallen. It was the same feeling I'd had the previous winter when I talked with Margaret Rawson, a complete loss of self and a touching of souls. I went to the dictionary to try to find words for it. *Mesmerize, hypnotize,* and *trance* weren't quite right, either.

In all my twenty years of interviewing, I'd rarely felt such intense emotions and lack of journalistic control during an interview. The only comparable experience had been with Holocaust survivors. I'd done some oral-history interviews for the United States Holocaust Memorial Museum and would often be shaken for days afterward. But it was not my role to make sense of those stories, only to facilitate their telling. But with the centenarians, I thought I had to keep control because I had to write about their lives for the radio series. It was confusing. Letting go felt good, losing control seemed wrong. Then a book came to me that helped me understand what was happening.

A friend recommended it—*A General Theory of Love,* written by three psychiatrists: Thomas Lewis, Fari Amini, and

Richard Lannon. It's an attempt to explain the biological basis of human emotions, especially love.

The doctors describe a phenomenon they call "limbic resonance." They say it's a "symphony of mutual exchange . . . whereby two mammals become attuned to each other's inner states. When we meet the gaze of another, two nervous systems achieve a palpable and intimate apposition." In other words, we have the ability to feel each other's emotions.

The doctors explain that the limbic region of the brain is unique to us mammals, who differ significantly from, say, reptiles, in that we care for our young. A snake can watch its offspring eaten by an eagle and not react; a mother bear, however, has a strong protective instinct.

This "orientation toward offspring" is where limbic resonance begins, they say. Because our babies are born defenseless, a mother must know the internal state of the infant, and indeed, has the ability to do so. It's hardwired into the brain. We all have it—men, too. But as we grow and move away from our mothers and into the world, which is full of distractions, we forget that we have this ability and, more important, we forget how much pleasure it brings us. There is nothing that makes us happier than feeling this connection with another human being. It is the biological basis of what we call love, a sensory ability just like sight or hearing or touch. It's also why we can connect with our dogs and cats and horses. They are limbic, too. Women, the doctors say, are often more aware of this than men.

This makes sense to me, that the feeling I was describing as "falling" was limbic resonance. I was feeling the emotional states of the centenarians, losing my own state and taking on theirs. And I am beginning to think that the centenarians know about this intuitively. They know how important the connection with others is, because it's harder for them to get it. They are often alone and understand that being cut off from other people is a death sentence. I think it explains why they're so quick to make a connection when someone comes along who's willing to offer it.

And maybe they're better at it, too, because they grew up in a world without so much distraction, when people were more likely to talk to one another—at the dinner table, around the fire at night, riding together in a sleigh, or walk-ing to school. The centenarians grew up in a world with no electricity: no radio to turn to when the conversation got dull or tense, no television to take the place of someone telling stories, no e-mail to check five times a day. Their world was more likely to be full of the sounds of nature, a place where you could think more clearly and perhaps connect with peo-ple more readily.

I decided that the doctors who wrote this book knew exactly what had been happening to me because it happened to them, too. There was a passage on page sixty-five of *A General Theory of Love* that I underlined:

> The vocation of psychotherapy confers a few unexpected fringe benefits on its practitioners, and the following is one of them. It impels participation in a process that our modern world has all but forgotten: sitting in a room with another person for hours at a time with no purpose in mind but

attending. As you do so, another world expands and comes alive to your senses—a world governed by forces that were old before humanity began.

I called one of the authors, Thomas Lewis, and told him I wanted to come and see him in September, when I'd be in San Francisco to interview another centenarian. He agreed.

IT'S HIGH SUMMER now, and my radio series is half over. Back in Indiana, my brother and sister and I throw a big party to celebrate my parents' fiftieth wedding anniversary. Relatives come from nearby Chicago and five other states. It's an emotional reunion. We watch old home movies of the wedding, and so many faces in those flickering memories are gone now. My dad cries as he tries to speak before the hushed group—which includes his 98-year-old mother—and tries to say how much he loves my mother. We watch them dance, clinging to each other in the dark as their favorite song fills the banquet hall and swirling specks of light glance off a mirror ball, spinning like the earth in black space.

A FEW WEEKS later, I'm standing beneath another mirror ball, in broad daylight, at Friendship Village, a senior living community in Schaumburg, Illinois, just west of Chicago. I've come to interview 104-year-old Helen Boardman.

"Delighted to receive your letter about an interview with me," she had written to me in an e-mail. "That's a subject dear to my heart."

The mirror ball hangs unnoticed today above the busy lobby at the heart of the Village. All eyes are focused on the dogs bouncing around on the carpet. It's Canine Companion Day. Community volunteers have brought their dogs so the seniors can pet and coo over them. There are lots of smiling people and smiling dogs, too.

Friendship Village is a place for active, independent seniors, and everyone here knows Helen Boardman, one of the most active and independent among them. My own interest in her was piqued when I found out she had remarried at age ninety-seven, to a man twenty years younger.

Bill Boardman comes bounding over to meet me in the lobby. He's wearing bright green slacks, a plaid shirt, and tennis shoes. He's lighthearted and beaming, insists on carrying my heavy bag as we head up a long corridor toward their apartment. Except for the handrail along the wall, it looks like a college dormitory.

Helen is waiting for us, chipper and smiling, too. You might guess that she's eighty-five. Her hair is short and curly and still naturally dark brown. Mine has more gray than hers.

She and Bill begin and end each other's sentences and ask a lot of questions. They're effervescent and funny. They can't wait to show me their apartment, the photos of their families, Helen's enlarger, the furniture Bill has made, Helen's books-on-tape, and the scrapbook of her life.

Finally we all calm down and Helen sits in a recliner, leaning forward to see and hear me better. She sends Bill to the other room. I find a low stool and sit close.

She was born and raised in an Illinois farming community called Hoopeston, about one hundred miles south of

Chicago. Her parents had ideas and needs that exceeded what small-town life had to offer, and so when Helen was four years old, around 1900, they started traveling to Southern California for the winter.

She remembers the train making stops to take on water and fuel. "They'd let everybody get off and the train would be waiting while we ate." And she remembers arriving in Southern California in the early morning.

"There were orange blossoms everywhere! We couldn't believe it was summer in California when it was cold and snowy in Illinois."

Helen's father got a winter job driving the electric Inter-Urban trains from the beach to downtown Los Angeles. In the spring they'd go back to Illinois. Every winter they'd come back and live someplace different—one year, near the corner of Hollywood and Vine.

"There were vacant lots with castor beans growing very high. Oh, how I wish my father had purchased a few acres," she says.

In the winter of 1906 they lived in Venice, near the beach, and she remembers feeling the earthquake that destroyed San Francisco. "Oh, wasn't that fun! I hope it does it again," she recalls saying and being chastised by her grandmother, who said, "It might be causing other people trouble."

Helen really does say "Oh" in conversation. She has a dramatic flair and perfect diction. Her mother was concerned about giving her children a proper upbringing, so young Helen had elocution training. She also remembers being taken to hear the famous opera diva Dame Nellie Melba in Los Angeles. "You may remember her from Melba toast," she says.

Every chance she got in Hoopeston as a child, Helen was performing. When Teddy Roosevelt came through town as a presidential candidate for the Bull Moose Party in 1912, she was asked to recite before the crowd "When You Hear the Bull Moose Roar." And when she was older, her mother sent her to the Leland Powers School of the Spoken Word in Boston, to prepare her for a life on the stage. There she learned to perform monologues, which, at that time, was considered an art form. But when she finished it was decided she needed more academic training, so she transferred to DePauw University and then the University of Illinois. By the time she finished college, practical realities had set in, and Helen taught for one year before she got married to Curtis Boardman, who'd been her high-school sweetheart. They were best friends, she says. They raised three kids, went to church, were scout leaders, hosted an exchange student, played bridge twice a month, spent a lot of time with their extended families, and sent all their kids to college. When Curtis Boardman retired after forty-three years with the American Can Company, they did some traveling for the first time in their marriage.

Curtis died in 1966 after suffering the effects of a stroke for a year. When he died, Helen was seventy years old, but she adjusted quickly. She moved from Hoopeston to Fort Lauderdale, Florida, and returned to school. "It was time to move on to another phase," she says.

"I guess I'm an optimist. I thought the best was ahead. I thought about that poem, 'Grow old along with me!/The best is yet to be/The last of life for which the first was made.' I had made provisions mentally for Curtis's death. I expected it. I knew the decisions I made would be right. I didn't hesitate to leave, even though I was living in the home where I was born. I had an opportunity then to do some of the things I wasn't able to do earlier because of family and other obligations."

Helen moved into Friendship Village when she was eighty-eight. She didn't want her children to have to care for her. She immediately got busy organizing drama productions, as she had done all her life. And soon she met Bill and Ellen Boardman, same last name. They kept getting each other's mail, and Bill was a handy Mr. Fix-it kind of guy who could build anything needed for the shows.

Ellen Boardman, Bill's wife, died suddenly, and within a year, Helen and Bill were joining each other at one function or another. In a couple of years, they decided to get married.

Bill interrupts our conversation to announce that it's time for lunch. They're eager to take me to the Friendship Village dining room. First, Bill reads aloud the menu for the day, which is posted on the refrigerator. Helen listens intently.

The dining room reminds me of a Midwestern Holiday Inn restaurant, as they were when I was a kid: vast. This one has wall-to-wall carpeting, tablecloths and napkins, upholstered chairs on casters. Men and women here are nicely dressed, some of the men in sports coats. There are lots of walkers parked around the room. It's a sea of white hair and stooped shoulders but lots of laughter and neighborly waving.

We go through the cafeteria-style lines, surveying the ravioli, beef stroganoff, cod, ratatouille, mashed potatoes, steamed vegetables, salad bar, fruit bar, and dessert bar. Today's special is strawberry shortcake. There is Jell-O, of course, green and red.

There's a uniformed wait staff and they carry our trays

to a table and assume we want coffee with our meal. We eat leisurely.

Helen and Bill are good storytellers and good listeners. Bill tells a lot of jokes and seems to feel responsible for keeping Helen and me laughing. All during lunch, people stop by to say hello; often the women give Helen a hug. Bill remembers all their names and says a kind thing to each of them. One fellow is the editor of the literary magazine, another works with Bill in the woodshop. Bill has brought a plastic bag full of tomatoes and a bouquet of zinnias from his garden for a woman who's delighted to get them.

On the way back to their apartment, we pass a gift shop in the hallway, a library, a post office. Bill and Helen are both outgoing, like celebrities, as we walk down the halls back to their apartment.

After lunch I settle down to interview them together.

Bill came to Friendship Village with his first wife, Ellen, when he was just seventy-three. He and Ellen had known each other all their lives; they grew up on the same street, much like Helen and her first husband, Curtis. Bill and Ellen came to Friendship for the same reason Helen came, so as not to be a burden to their children. When Ellen died, Bill had the same forward-looking attitude that Helen had when she lost Curtis. "You have to accept it and move on," he says.

"We see people here in the Village, it's hard on them, they can't accept the death of a partner. I don't know why we are the way we are, it's just our personalities."

Getting together was not a big deal, they both insist. It was actually harder for other people to accept.

When they started spending time together in one apartment, the Friendship Village management "took a jaundiced view of it," Bill says.

"You mean they called you in?"

"They thought it was immoral or something. The executive director decided it was improper. I said, 'You're crazy.'"

Bill was more worried about what the federal government would say.

"We were afraid that Helen's hospitalization would be null and void, so we called Social Security and they said it would make no difference, so we decided to get married.

"My children were a little startled to think I would marry someone much older, but when they met Helen, they could see it would be a good thing," Bill says. He was seventy-eight when he married Helen.

"We first announced to our children that we would elope, but they said, 'Oh, no, we're coming to your wedding.'"

"I've always wondered," I say, "is love a different feeling at your age or does it feel the same as when you're getting married at, say, twenty-one?"

Helen is serious. "Well, you're just really mature in every respect. You don't expect the romance you do when you're twenty. The passion is calmed down considerably. It's just real love and there's nothing to complicate it when you're our age. You just love the companionship of a relationship with another person that loves you. And that is so satisfying in your older age."

"It's a much calmer situation," adds Bill.

"Bill," I said, "didn't part of you say, 'What am I getting myself into?' It seems to me an extreme act of optimism to marry someone ninety-eight years old."

"That's right. Sure, I thought about it, but I'm inclined to be optimistic. She was in good health and I was, too. If one goes before the other, you can't worry about that. We didn't think of it as a deterrent. I should say not. We've had a wonderful life together. It's meant so much to both of us."

"I don't know what I would do without him," Helen says. "All the help he gives me. The little things you do automatically and don't think about are difficult for me now, like buttoning cuffs. Even cutting my fingernails and toenails."

"She gets a little whisker once in a while that has to be trimmed," Bill laughs. "But that's love. You do things like that for the person you love. That's what makes life interesting. We have fun despite a few difficulties."

Here is my chance to ask about sex, but I can't get the question out. I stumble around, asking about "intimacy" and "the joys of a relationship."

"Are you asking if we have sex?" says Bill.

"Well, yes."

"We've enjoyed sex. It's not the same as you would have when you're eighteen. It's restricted considerably."

Helen finishes the thought. "I enjoy having his arms around me just as much as I did when I was first married. You never get tired of that, and you miss it when you don't have it," she says.

Maybe I could have guessed those answers myself. You won't miss it. You don't need it. Hugging, though, you never get tired of that.

I'm sure Helen and Bill must argue sometimes, or have dreadful, complicated disagreements with their kids, like most people, but in the two days I spent with them, there was no hint of darkness in their lives, and by the end of our visit, I felt resilient and upbeat. Helen gave me a copy of the memoir she wrote before her hundredth birthday, called *99 and Counting: Helen's Journey,* and Bill helped me carry it, along with my bag, out to the parking lot.

I was charmed by his good humor, his optimism, his many enthusiasms, and his obvious devotion to Helen, and since Bill is merely eighty-four, and a diligent correspondent, I feel sure we will meet again soon.

That night I begin to read Helen's book. On page one she says she has no idea why she lived so long, but on the last page, I think, is the answer: "The chief joy of the future," she writes of her life with Bill, "is that it stretches ahead filled with things to do together."

IT'S A LATE August evening in Portland, Maine. Noah and I amble—uncharacteristically—down cobblestone streets. We linger in town, savoring the last hours of our annual vacation in Maine. We've been sailing Down East with dear friends, sleeping on a boat aptly named *Free Spirit,* swimming in the ocean and relaxing long enough to remember that we have dreams for the future. We aren't quite ready to go back to our city lives.

We find ourselves at the waterfront, on the quay as the ferry from Peak's Island approaches. An onshore breeze cools our windburned faces. We lean against the railing and see vacationers on board in their shorts and sandals, their hair tousled from the wind. They carry coolers, backpacks, and kids. It's a happy and timeless scene: A boat arrives on a summer evening, the sky is clear, and the silvery light—exquisite and clean—is fading to gold. People disembark and head home. We walk with them back toward town, uphill.

We turn off the street and climb granite steps into a familiar old building, perhaps an old ship chandlery, that now sells "maritime artifacts, curiosities and salvage." We seem to end up here every year. Noah tries on the same musty pea coats that didn't fit right last year; I admire the sextants, binnacles, and compasses, and fish my glasses out of my pocket to read the inscriptions on the old naval photographs.

There's a glass case on the wall. Rows of keys on cup hooks dangle and glimmer. My eye lands on a brass one, four inches long—a skeleton key with an elegant oval on the handle end. I reach up to open the door on the box and free the key from its hook. It lays across my palm, crossing my extra-long lifeline. It has weight and grace.

Noah comes up behind me and sees the keys, reaches up and finds a silver one, similarly long and heavy. The number 53 is stamped on the shank and a white plastic tag attached to the end is printed with nearly indecipherable words: ENG. R<u>M</u>. ENT. (UPP. P & S) He knows he has to have it. He turns and buys it without hesitating.

"Wait, I want this one, too," I say.

We leave the store and head home with our keys. They are beautiful keys and memorable. They journeyed across oceans, we suppose, from one world to another, opening doors or closets or trunks or lockers. Now they are ours. Today we don't know what they open, but someday we will.

14

THOMAS LEWIS

"The thing that will make you happy, nobody tells you."

IN SEPTEMBER I flew to San Francisco with my underlined copy of *A General Theory of Love*. Dr. Thomas Lewis, one of the three authors, had agreed to meet me and I was reading parts of it again at thirty thousand feet, reviewing my questions. I planned to ask him about the loss of control I'd felt in some of the interviews, about the falling sensation I'd had, and also about the deep feelings I've carried around afterward. And as I flew, I tried to get caught up in my journal, writing about the summer, the mail I've gotten from listeners, the news I'd gotten from centenarians, their families and friends.

Just before I left for San Francisco, I'd received an e-mail from Sarah Uhle, Ruth Ellis's friend:

Dear Neenah, I know you would want to know. Ruth is in the hospital. It may not be anything serious. We can't tell yet. It also might be the beginning of the end.

Ruth was found to have acute heart disease in addition to a number of chronic ailments. Sarah reported that Ruth's "girls" were caring for her and making plans for her care when she got out of the hospital, as she was keen to do. Someone had brought Ruth barbecued ribs the previous Saturday night, which she ate happily. Sarah's note was signed, "All of us loving Ruth and holding her in the light."

I VISIT DR. LEWIS the next morning at his office near the University of California's Parnassus campus. He has a sprawling, panoramic view to the north and east. He's younger than I'd guessed, energetic and soft-spoken. I explain to him again why I've come and I find he is an excellent listener. I can feel the focus of his attention and it feels odd. Usually I'm the listener. His attention makes me hear what I'm saying more clearly.

I ask him to talk about limbic resonance. The limbic part I understand; it comes from the limbic region of the brain, in mammals. It's the resonance part I'm intrigued with. Dr. Lewis says he's not sure he can define it, but he can describe it.

"We're familiar with traditional senses," he begins, "like your eyes give you information about electromagnetic radiation or your ears give you information about changes in sound waves. Well, there's another sensory system in the brain, which is designed to give you information about the emotional state inside someone else's brain, and that sensory experience is limbic resonance.

"Limbic resonance is a two-way path; you can sense the inside of someone else's brain, they can sense the inside of yours, and each person influences the other. It's a two-way sensory experience of emotion."

"Are there other terms for it?" I ask. "If it's such a basic human function, you'd think there would be."

"There are," he says. "The most common word I know for it is a *vibe*. You hear people talk about 'getting a vibe off someone.' People think that's an amusing, fantastic metaphor, but it is, I think, the literal truth, that really, you *can* get a vibe off somebody, and it's a completely legitimate sensory experience. *Vibe* is a good word because it carries the implication that you yourself are a little bit changed by the experience, that you can feel it and maybe you're tuning into it a little bit."

If this is true, and I've been feeling the emotional states of the centenarians, it explains a lot. Why, for example, I felt wary and nervous with Abe Goldstein, the law professor, from the minute he walked in the room—it was because he was wary. And why with R. L. Stamper, I felt the hair on the back of my neck tingle when he talked about the end of the world, even though I didn't believe it. He believed it deeply. Lewis's theory could explain why it felt so good to be around Anna, who was laughing and happy and couldn't wait to show me her lake.

But I've been losing control in these interviews, I tell Dr. Lewis, in a way that I never had before. Early on I'd given up asking questions from my list of the major events of the twentieth century, and in some interviews, I realize, I barely interacted at all. When I listened again to the tapes of the interviews, I was surprised at how little I'd said, even though my memories of the interviews were vivid. It seemed as if I'd given up trying to interview in favor of just having a conversation, and then given that up, too, content to just sit and listen.

I assumed Dr. Lewis would understand this and, since he's a psychotherapist, he could tell me how to gain con-trol again.

"But why would you want to?" he asks. "I'm sure that what you're doing to them plays a large part in what's happening. And one of the reasons I think that's true is because during the last year I've done a bunch of interviews about the book on TV and radio and in different kinds of settings, and one of the most interesting things to me, which I would never have anticipated, is that *regularly,* the quality of *my* thought in the interview is a direct product of the quality of the interviewer.

"For instance, it's pretty clear when you talk to somebody whether they've read the book or not, whether they understand the book or not, whether they're doing this because it's a job, or whether they're really interested in the subject, if it's really alive for them. And if it's not alive, if they are flat, perfunctory, or dull, I couldn't put life into it. And it frustrated me until I figured out what was going on. Either there's a resonance or there isn't, and if there is no resonance, then it's information that has no larger meaning, no depth to it. It was fascinating to me, because I couldn't really tell how an interview was going to go because it didn't really depend on what I knew about the subject. So I'm sure that just having been on the other end of interviews that it makes an enormous difference."

"Dr. Lewis, tell me what's happening in these interviews. You say there is an exchange between two people. What exactly is being exchanged?"

"Well, because people are mammals, they have this part of the brain that allows them to tune into the brain of another mammal. That's why if you look at a snake, you get no sensation that anything's happening, because that's a reptile and reptiles are pre-limbic, meaning they evolved before this part of the brain. When you look at another person you have that emotional connection. Usually it's eye contact that makes the connection or facilitates it, but it doesn't have to be. For example, we know that blind people and blind babies can have that contact, but usually it's initiated by vision. Your brain reads the facial expression, the pupil size, the body language, in an instant—in a microsecond—and gets a kind of snapshot of what's going on inside the other person's brain and adjusts a little bit toward that. At the same moment, the other person's brain does the same thing."

"Wait, what does that mean, 'you adjust toward it a little bit'? This is all a nonverbal, unconscious thing we're talking about, right?" I ask.

"Emotions or feeling states are contagious," he says, "because people have a natural tendency to detect the emotional state of the other person and align with it, or move a little bit closer to it. So if you're sitting with someone who's highly anxious, you yourself start to get a little more anxious than you were before. If you're sitting with someone who's terribly depressed, you align a little bit and you become a little bit down and morose.

"That's why people go to a movie theater to see a movie. Everybody else within range is simultaneously having the same emotion that you are and you get a magnification of the emotional experience. That's why movies are so much more intense than seeing something in your living room, alone.

"Everybody has an innate tendency to sense the inside of another person and to align themselves a little bit in that direction. So when you meet somebody, your brain does that and theirs does the same thing and you have brains that are aligning a little bit with each other. If they're compatible, they may align very much and people feel that—you can feel it on a gut level, and that's what they mean when they say they made a connection with somebody or there was 'chemistry' or they really felt bonded. There really *is* something happening between them. Does that make sense?"

"Yes, but what is it? Is it an electrical thing in your brain? Is it a chemical reaction?"

"Well, everything in your brain is electrical or chemical, so it certainly is that. How to say it . . . ? Say if I look at the chair: It looks black or angular, or there are shadows. But none of those things really exist; that's a virtual reality that my brain creates, out of tiny little pieces of data about electromagnetic radiation. And my brain's creation is what exists. There's no such thing as a chair looking angular or solid or black or silver or shiny or shadowy. The chair I see is a virtual reality that my brain constucts. The same thing is true about the connection that people have. Their brains are doing what they are supposed to do: align with each other. It's a process through which one brain tunes into another, aligns to it, another brain tunes into the first one, aligns, the original brain senses that alignment, changes a little bit itself, and so on. There's kind of a ricochet of alignment going back and forth. That's the process. What we experience is: 'Wow, this person gets it,' 'We're connected,' or 'We're bonded,' or 'We're linked,' or 'We're soul mates.' When you feel it, it's undeniable, it's like a key sliding into a lock, like *bam!* Does that make sense?"

It does make sense to me. It seems that I'm good at picking up on people's emotional states. My brain "aligns," in Dr. Lewis's words. I've been referring to it as "falling," and according to Dr. Lewis, it's not surprising that I've described it as a good feeling.

"You know," he says, "this is not a thought that's original with me, but it's a truth that keeps getting lost and people keep rediscovering it and people keep losing it: About the only thing that makes people happy is spending time with people they are emotionally close with. Other things don't make them happy; in fact, most of the things that our culture says should make you happy don't, like a Rolex or a condo in Vail, this kind of car or that kind of job. They just don't make people truly happy. The thing that will make you happy, nobody tells you very much, you kind of have to find it out on your own, if you're lucky.

"In the United States, what people are happy? The people who are happy are a lot of blue-collar families, a lot of families that are less than blue collar, the kind with strong family values, or whatever; they spend a lot of time together—having dinner together, playing football on the weekends together. They don't have the most glamorous jobs or cars or homes, they're not going to be executive vice president or anything else, but they're having a decent life and they're happy. I actually think you can't have both. I believe you can't have happiness and be at the top of your field or be the most accomplished person."

Surely, I suspect, he's overstating the case a bit to make a point. There are affluent people who are happily in touch with their families. Dr. Lewis admits that most of his patients are striving baby boomers, blinded by their own ambition, unable to find happiness at even the highest levels of income and power, but his point is a powerful one and I feel sure that most of the centenarians I've met would agree with him: Ruth Ellis, who's so worried about all the lonely seniors; R. L. Stamper, who's desperate to find a wife; and Helen Boardman, who found love again in her nineties. They haven't forgotten the importance of pure human, emotional contact the way many of us have, the way I often have.

I FELT ELATED after talking with Thomas Lewis. I went out into the city. The afternoon light was magic. The city was a living painting. The twisted pines on the UCSF campus were a revelation. My rental car was lovely, the local public radio station inspired, the weather, the traffic, the planets all in a cosmic alliance.

That evening, with all these ideas swirling inside, I walked from my hotel near Union Square to North Beach to meet my friend Eve for dinner. She's a high-spirited, open-hearted person, a former radio producer and psychotherapist. She's the kind of person you want to tell everything to. Now she's a dot-com vice president.

I told Eve about my "falling" experiences with the centenarians and the limbic resonance theory, too, and she immediately understood. "Oh, of course," she said. "And don't you know why therapists make their patients lie down on a couch? It's so they don't have to look into their eyes for so long. It's too intense. You'd get too attached."

I HUGGED EVE good-bye and headed back to my room. I had to walk and sort this out.

I wasn't falling in love with all the centenarians, but I was spending enough time with them to feel their emotions very deeply. I was sitting close to them and looking into their eyes for hours. If they were lighthearted, like Anna Wilmot and Helen Boardman, I felt great. If they were upset and lonely, like R. L. Stamper, I felt those things. Harry Shapiro, the painter, made me feel his hopeful introspection.

Now I realized that I had been putting myself in a vulnerable position by sitting so close, by staying so long, by not having an agenda. But what I had been thinking of as my passivity was making it easier for them to talk.

All my professional life, I've always wanted to be the talker, the performer, the author, the one at the center of the circle telling the story. Never mind that I'm not much good at it, that I can't even tell a joke very well. But now I was beginning to understand that my real strength could be as a listener.

15

MARION COWEN

"I just accept my life day by day."

THE NEXT MORNING at eight-thirty I'm knocking on an apartment door in Ocean Beach, across the street from the Pacific Ocean. I've come to interview 101-year-old Marion Cowen.

He was recommended to me by a social-service agency called Little Brothers/Friends of the Elderly. The group's mission is to relieve loneliness among San Francisco's huge population of elderly, a high percentage of whom live alone. Little Brothers matches up volunteers with elders for social visits and occasional outings. They've introduced me to Marion Cowen and a volunteer named Peter Carlson, who's been visiting Marion for nearly ten years. They've also sent me newspaper clippings about Marion.

GILDED CENTURY STUDDED WITH STARS, says a headline in the *San Francisco Examiner*, and there's a picture of Mr. Cowen seated on a piano bench, in front of two candelabra atop a baby grand. He's sitting sideways to the camera, hands clasped in his lap, head bowed, eyes crinkled with laughter. He has a sweet, elfin look and the long, graceful fingers of an artist.

The article says he remembers the 1906 earthquake and that he's trying to get a novel published. He thinks Matt Damon would be perfect for the role in the movie version of a novella he has written, and he has an idea for another book, too, called *The Loves of Sally*, about the eight husbands of San

Francisco's famous madam Sally Stanford, who was a friend of his. He's worked in theater in New York and Hollywood in the twenties and thirties. The folks at Little Brothers assure me he is a great storyteller.

Peter Carlson, the volunteer, comes to the door. He is eager for me to meet Marion and also seems to want to help him through his interview.

The apartment is small, just three rooms, and full of plants. A picture window frames a spectacular view of the ocean. The piano is in the corner, lid down, keys covered. The living room is disheveled, as if someone other than Marion has been living among his belongings.

Peter introduces me to a health-care aide who is preparing a meal in the open kitchen and then takes me into the bedroom.

Marion is lying in bed, pale against two clean white pillows. He's wearing silky, navy blue pajamas. The blanket is pulled up neatly to his chest, so all I can see are his head and shoulders, arms and hands, which are crossed on top of his chest. His fingers are at rest, the nails nicely shaped. He's almost completely bald. There's an open box of See's chocolates next to him on the bed.

"Well, hello," he says, his voice a little nasal.

"Marion, this is the reporter I told you about from public radio," says Peter.

"Oh! Well, I'm pleased to meet you."

I set up my tape recorder at his bedside and clip the microphone to his pajamas. Peter excuses himself and goes out into the living room.

"And what's the purpose of what you're going to do here?"

I tell him about the radio series. He's full of polite questions.

"And where does the broadcast emanate from?" he wants to know. "And what is the program called?" he asks. "Perhaps you'd like something before we start?"

I decline, eager to get going.

"And how long will you be staying in town?"

We get the small talk out of the way and I start in.

"Tell me about some of your earliest memories. What do you remember about being a little boy?"

"Well, I remember the earthquake and fire. I remember every detail of that, of course."

"What happened to your house?"

"Nothing happened. We were living in Oakland at the time. There was a breakage of china and that sort of thing. The chimney came down and that's about it. We weren't able to cook for quite a while. We had to cook on the street. Everybody had to keep running in and out, all the chimneys having come down. I don't remember *all* the details."

I'd read some of this story in that *Examiner* article about him.

"Your grandmother was living in San Francisco at the time," I say.

"Yes, I went with my mother to get her. The earthquake was early in the morning and we took the ferry across the Bay. My mother was a rather aggressive person and there was some talk of the ferry not proceeding across the Bay and she threatened to jump over and swim if the boat didn't proceed. Well, anyway, we got to the city and we walked up the cobblestone streets and we stopped at the Palace Hotel. My mother was the friend of the Baroness Kirkpatrick, who ran the Palace Hotel. Then we went to where my grandmother lived and got her."

"Did you see the fire?"

"Well, it was on its way. It hadn't gotten to that part of the city yet. My mother was able to hire a horse and buggy and driver, and we went around the edge of the city until we got to the ferry building and went back."

"Was your grandmother frightened?"

"Everybody was excited, but I don't remember anything specific that she said."

This was the great earthquake of 1906, the same one that Helen Boardman says she felt down in Los Angeles. Marion would have been nearly seven years old at the time. I figure he's told this story hundreds of times and as a result he sounds a little flat. I decide to go on to other subjects.

"How did you get interested in theater?"

"I played kid parts in two Oakland theaters. My mother had a friend who put me in shows whenever there were kids needed. One thing led to another."

"And how did you get to New York?"

"I went by ship. I was a stowaway by proxy. The captain arranged it."

"The captain hid you?"

"Yes, it was a freighter called the *Eastern Glade.*"

I'm beginning to wonder about his memory. He's leaping from fact to fact without telling stories. Some facts are like stepping stones in a creek. He can see them and he can get to them, but he can't describe the creek. It's too indistinct.

"When did you get to New York?"

"Well, let me think. I was in my late teens, so it would have been the twenties."

The math isn't quite right, but never mind.

"Did you know anyone in New York when you got there?"

"Mrs. David Belasco. She was my father's cousin and it worked out very well."

David Belasco was a famous and eccentric theater producer and playwright in the early part of the century. He was known for lavish productions with what we would now call special effects.

"What was it like in New York then?"

"It was very different from what I was used to. My father was a cousin to Mrs. David Belasco. I looked her up and one thing led to another. She helped me and I got jobs with various producers and that's how I got into the theater."

"Was it a dream of yours to work in the theater in New York?"

"I worked at it and that's what happened. My father was a cousin of Mrs. David Belasco. Her mother was my grandmother's sister."

"What kinds of productions did you work on in New York?"

"Oh, I'd have to do a lot of thinking about that. Just the regular Broadway plays, different plays."

"I understand you were a director."

"I knew David Balasco very well, of course. His wife was a cousin of my father."

We'd been talking only about fifteen minutes and it wasn't working. I'd gotten the impression from the newspaper article I'd read and from all the people I'd talked to that he's great at telling stories. But I must have come on an off day. I'm not hearing stories and I'm starting to throw questions at him randomly, hoping to find a subject he warms to, but I'm just making it worse. He's getting confused.

And then, luckily, Peter Carlson comes in. He's overheard us in the other room and he knows we've lost our way. He brings me a few pages of biographical material about Marion that he's highlighted. He's gentle and tactful, not wanting to alarm Marion, just trying to help me get the stories he's heard so many times.

"I've heard so much from Marion about the theater," Peter says to me. "Marion, did you like *Guys and Dolls*?"

"Didn't have anything to do with it," Marion says.

Peter turns back to me. "He hated *Guys and Dolls*."

I glance over the pages Peter has handed me.

"You were in Hollywood in the 1930s," I say to Marion.

"I don't remember. It seems likely, though."

Marion is losing interest in my questions and I can't blame him. I have met so many centenarians who are mentally sharp and I'm flustered because he's not. I stop asking the questions that are taxing him and get onto a more general, personal train of thought.

"Did anyone in your family live to be a hundred years old?"

"I don't think so. Certainly not my parents."

"How do you feel, Marion?"

"Oh, I feel all right. I'm not too much aware of my age. I know it's there, but it's nothing I speculate about."

There's a long pause as he looks far away.

"I'm sorry you have to dig so deep to get anything," he says wistfully. "I just take things every day as they come."

"Do you have family members alive?"

"No."

"Did you have brothers and sisters?"

"No, I've always been isolated."

"Did you *feel* isolated?"

"I never thought about it. Oh, I'm making you dig for everything."

"That's okay," I say, and let several moments pass. "I see you have a box of chocolates there." He hasn't touched them since I came in.

"I don't know a thing about it."

Marion is drifting away; his energy is fading and I feel it. He's like a flickering candle.

"Marion, you have a beautiful view of the ocean here," I say weakly.

"Well, I don't look out on it very often," he says. "When do you go back?"

"I think tomorrow."

"So soon," he says.

At just that moment, I'm ready to turn off the tape recorder when a cat jumps up on the bed, purring loudly, heading for Marion in long strides.

"Oh! Soho!" Marion comes to life. "He's such a great guy. He really fulfills his responsibility. He takes a great interest in everything that goes on here. He's not just an ornament."

"You're lucky to have a cat," I say.

"Oh, yes! And he's very understanding and sympathetic. He has an idea that he has to take care of me to an extent."

"You think so?"

"Oh, I'm sure of it. He's a real personality. He lives his own life and he does what he wishes." Marion is stroking the big, bony, long-haired Siamese. "He's pretty smart. He takes over as far as I'm concerned. He's got a proprietary interest in me."

"You belong to *him*," I say.

"Oh, yes, very much so."

Hoping to pick up on this new energy, I ask some new questions.

"Marion, do you get out very much?"

"Occasionally. Whenever it happens."

"Do you leave here to go to the doctor?"

"I don't have a doctor. Don't need one. I just accept my life day by day. I get out of here a lot, though."

"You do?"

"Oh, yes, sure."

"You can walk okay?"

"Oh, yes. I don't know why I'm lying in bed today. I don't have to do this. It just happened. I'm staying in bed but I really don't have to. I seem today to have landed here," he says. "What are your plans now?"

"Well, tomorrow I catch a plan and go home."

I remember the newspaper article about Marion, describing his novels and the musicals he's written, and I remember thinking I'd ask him to play the piano. That seems impossible now.

"I'd like to ask you about the musicals you've written. Can you tell me about those?"

"Not a lot. I certainly revised a number of them. I don't know that I could claim authorship. I haven't thought of these things in a long time."

"Is it hard to recall some things?"

"Well, I haven't tried, I can't say," he says. "And when do you leave?"

"Tomorrow."

"Oh!" he says, adding a dramatic little intake of breath. "So soon!"

Finally I understand that he is asking me to leave. Peter Carlson comes in and tries to help, asking Marion a few more questions he thinks could lead to some good stories, but it isn't working for him, either.

Peter hands me a stack of papers as I leave, biographical material about Marion, more newspaper articles, and samples of his writing. I thank Marion and Peter and leave. Actually, it's more accurate to say I flee, feeling strongly that Marion is near death.

I can't wait to get far away.

Back downtown near Union Square, I go for a walk. The noon crowds are moving fast along the sidewalks.

As is my custom, whenever I think I've screwed up, I have to take some time to tell myself how stupid I've been. What an idiot. Why didn't I call Marion ahead of time? I might have spared him the anxiety I caused.

At a café, I read the papers Peter has given me. There's an

interview with Marion's doctor. He told me he has no doctor. There are synopses of musicals he has written, eight of them, a series called *Queen of Nevada* about a Scottish lass named Eilley Orrum. The first scene begins with "a weird, fantastic night scene of revelry on a wooded heath with faeries, pixies and elves led by the Kind Kelpie." In subsequent chapters, Eilley moves to frontier America, marries a Mormon, and discovers the Comstock silver lode. At one point, Eilley "shines in the brilliance of her spectacular hoopskirt balls," and near the end, "laughter and admiration of everything prevails."

I leaf through the synopses and marvel at the sheer amount of work and the colorful imagination that produced them. It must have taken years to write all these. Marion's bio is four pages long. Opera. Theater. Novels. Radio plays. Television scripts and poetry, including *Too Much Is Not Enough*, "a collection of bizarre, zany verses." Marion wrote travel books about California, and worked as the head reader for Warner Brothers, selecting manuscripts with movie potential. It was a fascinating, if not totally illustrious, career. I'm surprised and impressed at how prolific he was.

But some things here contradict what he told me in the interview. I don't know what's real.

I call Peter from a pay phone on the street, to see if he will help me fill in the gaps. We make a plan to meet later in the day.

I walk back to the hotel through Union Square. A young woman is singing into a microphone at the edge of the park. She is solemn, arms at her side, with long, light hair, a T-shirt, no bra, a long skirt. She is singing about being homeless and lonely, asking these affluent strangers for money. Her voice is brittle and pretty. I can't take my eyes off her.

"Will you remember me tonight?" she sings.

I think of my conversation with Dr. Lewis about how emotional connection with another person is all that will make you happy.

"Will you remember me tonight?" the woman asks the indifferent tourists, declaring her loneliness to the world.

I leave her some money but I'm still a wide-open nerve after my talk with Marion, and I suddenly fill with remorse at my own failure to reach out to him. This young girl's pain wafts over the crowds like a blue mist.

My deepest fears rise up. Will I be alone and lonely when I am old?

"MARION'S EXISTENCE is pretty much what you saw today," Peter Carlson is telling me. "Sometimes I'll ask him what it's like and he says, 'I lead a pretty quiet existence. I live like a clam.' This morning before you arrived, Marion asked me how old he was. He wanted to remember for you."

"How is it that he's able to live alone?" I ask.

"There are three different gentlemen who come during the week through some kind of city agency," Peter explains. "Somebody comes every day but Marion is alone during the evenings."

"Is there someone who is legally responsible for him? Who will be there to make any medical decisions that might have to be made?" I ask.

"Well, if there's anyone, it would be his long-term friend Paul. Their affairs have been intermingled for a long time."

This suggestion of a relationship is a surprise. Marion never mentioned Paul—or anyone else—and the more I talk with Peter, the better I understand that Marion Cowen has lost his hold on life. He's teetering between this world and the next.

16

RUTH ELLIS III

"I just want to get out of this world."

I WAS AGITATED and overstimulated when I got back from San Francisco. Everything seemed vivid to me. As I walked in our neighborhood on a warm Sunday afternoon, the sound of crickets simmered steadily and I thought I could hear each one individually.

And then, a few days after my return, on October 5, Ruth Ellis died. The e-mail from Sarah Uhle was brief:

> This morning between 6:00 A.M. and 6:30 A.M. Ruth drifted off in her sleep. She was very peaceful. We're very grateful that she was able to go the way she had always wanted: at home, with friends, without a lot of hoopla.

Two weeks later I was sitting in a church pew in downtown Detroit, a few blocks from Ruth's apartment.

"Look around you," said a minister. "This is the rainbow community Ruth Ellis created."

The church was full of women and men, children, teenagers, senior citizens, gay couples, and row after row of Ruth's girls.

"Ruth gave us a vision of how the world could be. She would say, 'Tell everyone that I love everyone.'"

The crowd affirmed this to be true.

" 'I'm just an ordinary person,' Ruth would say."

Everyone had heard Ruth say this.

"Just look at the power of what ordinariness can do!" Smiles all around. Speaker after speaker, old friends and ministers and people who worked at the senior centers that Ruth loved, told their favorite Ruth stories.

"She would strut down the aisle in church, giving us her royal wave and saying, 'Don't forget the seniors!' " a woman from the senior center at the church remembered. "At her hundredth birthday, we gave her one dollar for every year of her life. Two weeks later she made a two-hundred-dollar donation to the center."

Dorothy Rutkowski, a longtime friend, stood solemnly. She was tall and fair and soft-spoken, with a wise, easy smile. "I am one of Miss Ruthie's children," Dorothy said. "She had many families." And Dorothy revealed that once, at a dance, she and Ruth got married by jumping the broom.

Jaye Spiro, the woman who had introduced Ruth to the white lesbian community of Detroit twenty years earlier, told about Ruth's 101st birthday party the previous July. There was a big cake. "Ruth looked at it," said Jaye, "and said, 'I hope there won't be any more of these.' "

There were gospel choirs, a violin solo, and poems declaimed. At the end of the service, a women's drumming group led the way out of the sanctuary and up the stairs to the fellowship hall. Everyone was laughing and clapping and agreeing that Ruth would have loved it.

A few hours later I found myself downtown, in a festive

Greek restaurant with seven other women, all wanting to talk more about Ruth.

Sarah Uhle told about the last days of Ruth's life, how she told the women who were caring for her that she was going to show them "how to die scientifically." Once she got out of the hospital, Ruth had quit eating, eager to "make her transition," as she called it.

Sarah's roommate Carolyn Lejuste wanted to tell about Ruth's last bath.

"Ruth loved the tub, she loved to soak."

Carolyn works with disabled people, so she knew to get in the tub with Ruth and hold her up while Sarah bathed her.

"It was a beautiful moment. I said to Ruth, 'This is a memory for me,' and Ruth said, 'Memories, memories, memories. It's all just memories now.'"

For a few days after that, Ruth lay in her own bed, passing in and out of consciousness. There were people with her twenty-four hours a day. She instructed them to take notes, "because it's history." A journal was kept.

October 1, 2000

Ruth woke up and said she wants to tell everyone she loves everyone, and wants it on her answering machine that she loves everyone. She told Mary Parker this morning that she didn't want people to ask how she feels because she feels bad and she's not going to get better.

At 11:00 she asked to be raised up. She says she doesn't

think she is sleeping. She did not want a drink when Mary tried to wet her lips with some Ensure. Got agitated that anything was going in her mouth.

At 11:15 Jeanne came out to report that Ruth told her she has "a plan. I don't want anybody touching me. Don't pet me. You can just go in the other room."

At 12:30 Ruth said, "Everything is scientific now. You even have to die scientifically." She said that's what she's doing, and laughed.

At 2:35 she said, "I'm having too much company." Ruth is aware of our presence when we look in at her. She opens her eyes but does not act like she really wants anyone in the room.

At 2:55 she said, "I don't know what they're doing to me. I can't sleep. Seems like I should have been out of here long ago. I don't understand why I can't sleep."

3:10—"Ruth Ellis, Ruth Ellis, it's Ruth Ellis. There's something wrong. I don't understand why I can't make the transition. I just want to make the transition and I can't."

4:25—Asked Mary Parker if she was going to stay all night. When Mary said yes, we are not leaving you, she replied, "Good, as long as someone is here."

4:35—"Oh, come on, they have got my sex all mixed up. They think I'm a man but I'm not. Have you checked the computer?" She smiles.

"They're not doing it right at all. I'm all messed up. They've been thinking I was a male and I'm not. I'm supposed to have been gone. It didn't work. I don't know whether you can understand what I'm saying. I'm supposed to have made the transition but I didn't . . . I'm going back, back, back . . . I don't want to keep anybody behind me that wants to get out. I'm all mixed up. I think I'm one place and I'm not. I can't hear what they say."

5:35—"I knocked them out, I tired them out."

Midnight—"I just want to get out of this world."

17

ROY LARKIN STAMPER II

"If we live together six months or a day, at least we're together."

SIX DAYS PASS. It's a Friday morning and I'm staring out the window, doing what freelancers do, looking at the bird feeder. The phone rings. "Thought you'd like to know that R. L. Stamper is getting married tonight."

It's a friend of Stamper's, a preacher I met last spring in Tulsa.

Twenty-five minutes later I'm on my way to the airport, contemplating the possibility that this is a miracle.

Delayed by weather, I arrive at the Stamper ranch at ten P.M., having missed the wedding ceremony. R. L.'s son Claude and some friends are calmly playing cards at Claude's kitchen table. I can't tell if he's happy or not.

"You wanna see the bride and groom?"

He takes me next door, just as he did five months ago, when I first visited.

A short woman is standing at the open refrigerator, the light pouring out onto her ice-blue dress. She turns toward me.

"Oh, I know who this must be! You're public radio!" she says, and gives me a hug.

Josephine Williams is the bride of R. L. Stamper and, it turns out, a public radio listener. She heard Stamper speaking over the radio last summer.

"And I thought, My, what a man. I need to know more about him."

So she tracked him down.

"I called him up and said, 'I'm a born-again Christian,'" and they started corresponding. He asked her to send a photo and then, in September, sent her airfare to come for a visit.

"What interested you about him?" I asked.

"It was mainly that he was a man that served his God and wanted the salvation of sinners," she said.

We go into the back room, where R. L. is getting ready for bed. He's stripped down to a T-shirt, trousers, and boots.

"Well, helllooooo." He is animated but seems tired. He reaches out both hands toward me. I kiss his cheek. He still smells like Aqua Velva.

They try to get me to eat some wedding cake, but we are all exhausted. I promise to come back in the morning.

R. L. is finishing breakfast as I arrive. Josephine is fussing over him and he's grinning. She is chatty and spirited. Her voice is high and warbly. She has a gracious Southern accent. She's from Shreveport, Louisiana. She is a strikingly beautiful woman, with white hair and light blue eyes. She's eighty years old.

"Were you looking to get married?" I ask.

"No! I had been a widow for twenty years. I had not really dated men, I thought that wasn't in God's plan. I just met a man who was different from any man I'd ever known! You're supposed to *know* when you speak with a man of God, you *know* that—God intends for us to bear witness. I *knew* this was a good man, a God-fearing man. I didn't have any idea whether we were gonna be friends when I called him. You know, it is true that you can love again, and it's also true that it doesn't have anything to do with how old you are."

I turn to her new husband. "R. L., when I was here last spring and you told me you were looking for a companion, did you think it would happen?"

"All things is possible. God was in the whole arrangement. *He* picked her out for me. I take Him in consideration. I wouldn't go to the mailbox without God. I want Him in our marriage. You know, people that prays together stays together."

"R. L., what did your family say when you told them you wanted to get married?"

He grins. "Well, one of them died and the rest got real sick, but we kept praying till they all gave in and were willing to accept her."

"They were concerned—"

"Concerned for my welfare. You don't know what I'd get into. They were afraid someone would take advantage of me and get my quarter. You know, I've got a quarter saved up." He winks. "They thought of everything that would happen but the *right* thing. I said to my son, 'Whatever *you* bring in here, if it's a black woman, I'll accept her. Will you do the same with me?' And he said, 'Well, yes.' 'And will you be good to her?' I asked him. And he come to in about an hour and I said, 'All right, I'm gonna get married,' and I think everything's all right now.

"If we live together six months or a day, at least we're together and not alone and *that's something*," he continues.

"You gotta have *somebody*. I would have liked a Seeing Eye dog, just anything! Well, she's better than a Seeing Eye dog and I thank God. I'm thankful that we found each other."

R. L.'s last wife, his third, died fourteen months ago after a long illness and he's been having a rough time alone. "A woman gets along better alone than a man," he says. "They's used to the house."

"Josephine, what did your children say when you told them you were getting married?"

"Well, they didn't just immediately say, 'That's okay.' They wanted to know about him. They weren't sure I wasn't coming into a cult. Well, it's not a *cult*. There's nothing like that here. It's a ranch. It's different, but it's not a cult!"

"You mean they were concerned that there was a reli-gious thing going on here."

"Yes, something I was being *swept into*. They were just curious. They didn't hear the interview the way I did. You know, people don't always get the same impression. I believed he was a man of God. I wouldn't be here if he were not."

"Amen," says R. L., smiling. "She's pretty small but she's all mine!"

"Did you sign prenuptial agreements?"

"Oh, yes," says Josphine.

"And everybody's cool with that?"

"Oh, yes. You know, there are five generations of Stampers here. These people all work together. This is their business—R. L.'s son, his grandsons. This should go on and I expect it to. I didn't marry him for monetary reasons. This should all stay in his family. I didn't marry him expecting his property to go to my people. But I believe he'll take care of me. I know this man will care for me the best he can."

"With God's help," says R. L. "I'm duty bound. So help me. I'll do it."

LATER THAT DAY I find myself driving west and laughing. I'm driving R. L.'s blue Cadillac, just as last spring I imagined I might if I were twenty years younger. Mr. Stamper and I are in the front seat chatting as we head into Tulsa for a luncheon. In the rearview mirror I see Josephine, nodding to sleep, feeling safe in the hands of relative strangers.

18

LOUISIANA HINES II

"It means something to do good.
It does. It means something."

BY EARLY NOVEMBER I was nearing the end of the radio series. I had two profiles to go. It was getting harder to choose whom I would interview. I had lots of tempting suggestions from listeners, but in November I chose to go back to Detroit and talk again with Louisiana Hines. Our interview the previous spring felt incomplete—I hadn't put it on the radio. Now I thought I could connect better with her.

Her granddaughter Darlene agreed to arrange things.

When I arrived, Mrs. Hines was at the stove, frying chicken wings in a skillet.

"You know my mother was called Cookin' Callie," she said. "She'd cook all kind of food for you. All *kind* of food." She promised to wrap up some chicken for me later.

I was feeling better than I had last time I was here, more relaxed, and I think she was, too.

We went into the living room and sat where we'd sat the previous spring. Now a Christmas tree was standing in front of the fireplace. It was decorated with white Styrofoam egg cartons hung on the branches, the bottoms carefully cut out of each egg cup. She had made them all herself.

"What did your mother do to get ready for Christmas?" I asked.

"She started cooking a few days before and she could cook up I don't know what 'n' all and have it ready for you.

She cooked cakes and pies and things like that. But her cakes pretty well be cooked the first of the week, you know. She'd cook pound cakes and she didn't measure. And her cakes would be just as smooth as you see 'em now. And she had plenty of butter and eggs and everything. And she had a sifter—she sifted the flour by shakin' it like that. They didn't have it like they do now."

Mrs. Hines had grown up on a farm in southern Alabama. Her parents were both the children of former slaves.

"I don't know," she continued. "People a long time ago, they didn't go by no cookbook, but your food was better, in a way of speakin', than it is now, you know. It would just be nice, and it didn't spoil like food spoils now."

"Is that right?"

"Mmm-hmm."

"In those days, did you have a Christmas tree?"

"Say what?"

"A Christmas tree, like you do now."

"Oh, yeah. But our Christmas tree wasn't like it is now. We'd go down in the woods and get holly bushes and cedars. And our houses wasn't made like they is now. They'd be cracks, you could stick the end of the limbs in that. Then the newspapers, we'd cut up into small, different sizes—some wide, some smaller than others—and we'd take flour and make a paste, because we didn't have glue, and we'd link those together and then we'd throw that over that and let it hang all over. Chains be hanging all over that. Then we would go down the road and get red clay and get white clay and wash the fireplace with white clay, and then we'd take the red clay and make designs all in that, uh-huh. And then white sand would be just like flour almost and we'd throw that all down on the fireplace, and you know, at that time it was beautiful. They didn't have the things they have now. They couldn't do what they do now."

She patiently described her mother's work: what laundry day was like, how she beat the clothes in a big black pot with a "battling stick," ironed them with starch they made themselves, made sausage, kept the garden, smoked meats. She was proud of her parents and had vivid memories of her grandparents, too. I was still especially interested in hearing what she knew about their lives as slaves.

Her grandparents were slaves on a plantation not far from where she grew up, owned by a man named Jack Bimbo, who, she was told, never beat his slaves, like other slave owners did.

"Sometimes they'd put them over a barrel and beat them, but Jack wouldn't allow that, and when they'd have their frolic, he said, 'They done worked, they can go off and enjoy theirselves.' He let them dance and do what they want to do. My granddaddy would just whoop the floor; he could dance, whoa, he could dance.

"He said all the time, 'Bimbo was a good man.'"

"Did you know your grandfather?" I asked.

"My granddaddy? Oh, yes, yes, yes. I'd sit on his knees and he'd talk to me so many times. I was with him when he passed. He used to tell me how he was gonna pass when the time come and everything. And I'd say to myself, 'I wanna see how it's gonna be done.' He said, 'I'm not gonna die, I'm gonna just *sleep away*,' and that's the way he did, too. I was the last one he talked with. He said, 'We're winded up, hon, just like a clock, and tickin' out.' He said, 'I'm tickin' out. I'm tickin' out now, it's gettin' shorter and shorter. And ain't nobody wind it up but Jesus, but it's tickin' out.' He said, 'I'm goin' where Lady is'—he called his wife Lady. He said, 'I'm goin' on away now, don't cry. Poppa goin' to rest.'"

I asked Mrs. Hines to tell me some of the stories she told me last spring. I wanted to hear more of everything. The stories flowed smoother the second time. I think we were both more comfortable. She had a better sense of what I was up to and I was paying better attention. She told me again the story of her mother's cousin George Teague, who was lynched for preaching that blacks and whites were equal in God's eyes. She remembered again how the whites killed Teague, "drug him around," and then came after his children, too. "We don't know what went with those boys."

"They disappeared," I said.

"They were *small* boys, *little* boys, but we don't know what happened. And this little girl, Rosie, when they come back, a white lady said she was so pretty, they didn't want to kill her. Said, 'Don't bother her, let her alone.' But them little brothers, we don't know, the folks always think that they destroyed 'em somewhere and they might have throwed them in that river. It wasn't far from Blue Creek. They never did see 'em no more. They were young children, size like that."

She held out her hand, palm down, and spoke softly.

"But they said they couldn't equal them because they was white, mmm-hmm."

"When you were growing up, were you afraid of white people?"

"No, I ain't never been afraid of white people. No. Mmm-hmm. Uh-uh. I ain't never been afraid." And then her voice got stronger, louder. "I'm not a 'fraid person. That's the reason I can stay by myself. I ain't afraid of nobody. I ain't afraid of you."

"But when you would hear those stories like that . . . ?"

"Mmm-hmm. I wasn't afraid. I don't know how come."

"Were other people afraid?"

"I don't know."

"Were your parents?"

"I don't know. They didn't say nothing about it, uh-uh. Now, my daddy wasn't a 'fraid person, but nobody would say that he was no *mean* person, either. Down there you could get ammunitions—as much as you want for little or nothing—and he had plenty of all kinds: cradle blades, pistols, muzzle loaders, and straight guns. Now, he would shoot these things and he taught us how to shoot."

"Oh, he did?"

"Oh, yeah. But he prayed to God that you'd never have to use that. If you have to do that, you have to do it. But if you don't have to do it, don't do it. And he had *guns,* honey."

When I asked Mrs. Hines if she was afraid, I was thinking about what it must have been like to live in the countryside, knowing that white people could come at any moment to your home and falsely accuse you, take you away, and kill you.

I had recently read a book by another centenarian, named George Dawson, called *Life Is So Good.* Dawson grew up in South Texas, but his grandparents had been slaves in Mississippi. He witnessed a lynching as a child, too, of a young man he knew well named Pete. And he remembered the fear he felt, knowing that members of the Ku Klux Klan were around.

"It was an awful thing to see them riding through in white robes with torches burning, guns shooting up the sky," he writes. "We didn't see them every day, but we could always feel them about."

It was this kind of general fear I had in mind when I asked Mrs. Hines if she was afraid, but she was thinking about a different kind of fear, a personal fear. She said, as if it needed to come out, "I ain't afraid of *you*."

At that moment, I felt a shift in our relationship. I felt closer to her, connected. I spent the whole day with Louisiana Hines, and when I left I think we both felt a warmth we had not felt before.

When I left for the airport, she wrapped some fried chicken wings in tinfoil for me and I ate them while I waited on my delayed flight at the Detroit airport. I sat and watched some lawyers arguing on CNN about what ballots should be counted in Florida. I licked my fingers and looked around, certain that no one else in this gate area was eating fried chicken made for them by a hundred-year-old woman.

A MONTH LATER, shortly after my interview with Mrs. Hines was on the radio, I got a letter from a lawyer in Washington, D.C., named Lairold Street. He'd spent years tracing his family's history in southern Alabama, and he thought he might be related to Mrs. Hines. He sent me some articles he'd written and I began to understand how difficult it could be for black Americans to trace their family history and how valuable the recollections of a centenarian could be. I put him in touch with Mrs. Hines.

A few weeks later, as we chatted at his home in Washington, I told Mr. Street about my conversation with Mrs. Hines and how she'd told me she wasn't afraid of me.

"Of course, it would be harder for her to talk to you than to me," he said. Apparently she had painted a much darker picture of her grandfather's experiences when she talked with Mr. Street.

"It's hard for the races to talk together about slavery," he said. "There's such a long history of mistrust." How could she have known that I would believe her stories? Maybe I wanted to believe that slave owners were not cruel. How could she know?

The truth is that I hadn't stopped to think about how she might react to me, a white stranger, coming into her home and asking her to share painful stories about her family's past. Maybe that explains why she was so nervous the first time we met and why she seemed to be going out of her way to tell about the good deeds of white people she had known, even as I kept asking for the ugly stories.

It's more important to remember the kindness of people, she seemed to be saying. "It means something to do good," she said. "It does. It *means* something."

Mrs. Hines is not worried about the past. She's thinking about the future, the day when Jesus comes.

"I think about it a lot of the time," she said. "We're on borrowed land. We're here for a short while. I don't care what they do with me. Just dig a hole and put me down there. Get one of these old pasteboard boxes. I don't want to be burnt, though."

"You don't want to be cremated?" I asked.

"No! I'm trying to stay *away* from the fire. You can call it creamed or stewed or pickled or preserved—anything— baked or boiled, I don't want it! Dig me a hole and stick me in the dirt.

"And don't go to no trouble carrying me nowhere, and don't dress me up all kinda way," she said. "Just come on and meet me there."

19

HARRY BOEFF

"Gee, I'm really telling you everything, aren't I?"

CHOOSING THE centenarian to end my series was surprisingly simple. He came to me in an e-mail from his neighbor. The subject line said, "My Centenarian."

> My next door neighbor, Harry Boeff, turned 100 on October 2. He has lived on this street since 1926. He has always been a model of what it means to be a good neighbor and is still today, an inspiration to all who meet him. He is known as the Mayor of Belmont St., as his home, front porch or back yard (weather the deciding factor) is always open and welcoming to tell stories, dispense advice or share in the famous "Boeff Beauties," raspberries that he grows in his back yard.

I was immediately attracted by the fact that he had been in one place for so long. I went to Rochester, New York, to see Harry Boeff. It was late November.

The sky was low and gray as I drove east along Lake Ontario from Buffalo. I know about "lake effect" snow, having grown up on the southern shore of Lake Michigan. These roads could easily be covered in shifting dunes of snow by morning.

I found Mr. Boeff's neighborhood on the southeast side of town and gave myself a quick driving tour to get oriented.

There was a city park nearby with lilac bushes taller than I am along its perimeter and a strip of restored storefronts at the south end of Belmont Street with some buildings dating from the nineteenth century. Some of the houses on Belmont Street itself were three stories tall—stout, square houses with open space between them and mature trees in front. They had wide front porches and neat backyards with wooden, detached garages and alleys across the back. It looked familiar to me, like small towns in Indiana.

Mr. Boeff's next-door neighbor, Barbara Mosher, who had sent me the e-mail, welcomed me into her cozy home. Her Old English sheepdog, Pandora, was friendly and sweet-smelling. Her husband, Ralph, came up from his woodshop in the basement. They offered to show me a videotape of Mr. Boeff before they took me next door to meet him.

A local television crew had come to Mr. Boeff's house during his hundredth birthday party to "take you from the dawn of one century to another."

The reporter asked Mr. Boeff the one question any reporter would ask who's only planning to stay a few minutes: What's the secret to living this long?

If you don't have all day, if you've got to get three minutes on that night's broadcast, you would have to ask this question. But Mr. Boeff knows you can't answer that question in one sentence and so he gives his shortcut answer and goes for the laughs: "Stay away from doctors and eat a lot of junk food."

MR. BOEFF IS waiting for us. He opens the heavy front door and he's smiling.

"Come on in. Where's the baby?" he says to Mrs. Mosher. He means the dog, Pandora.

He's neatly dressed in a brown-and-white-plaid flannel shirt with the neck buttoned up and a black cap with a gold insignia from the office of the county district attorney, which he also wore in the TV interview.

He takes me into the high-ceilinged kitchen for a drink of water. In the refrigerator I see apples and cans of cola and a vitamin drink called Boost. He sends me into the pantry to get a glass. The dishware is orderly, the glasses upside down. When I come back he declares, "Now you know where every-thing is, so you can make yourself at home."

He is easy to be with, sunny and open. He hears well and sees well. He moves easily, though he says he's stiff. He is slender and fair. I can't see his hair under the cap, but I guess it could be red or blond. I feel lucky and excited as we move to the living room.

He insists that I sit in his recliner, which faces the TV. It's his command post. There's a phone here and the remote control. From this spot he can see the front sidewalk and street on his left, and through the dining room to the back-yard on his right. He gently lowers himself onto the couch.

Harry Boeff—it's pronounced "Buff"—was born in Rochester in 1900, the fourth of six children. His parents were German immigrants. His father was a bookbinder. When Harry was seven, his mother died. In the next few years, his three older siblings moved away, then his father remarried and announced they were moving to Detroit.

Harry did okay there, he says. His stepmother was lov-ing, he had a lot of friends, and he was close to his younger brother, Bill. But three years later, his father wanted to move to Chicago. Harry begged to stay behind. He would work, he said, he could take care of himself.

"I told him I could peddle papers to make a living. They thought they'd give me a chance, to see what I could do. And Bill said, 'I want to stay with Harry,' so we started out, Bill and I, and we did it from age fourteen to seventeen."

Harry got a job delivering packages for a downtown haberdashery called Capper and Capper for five dollars a week. It was a swanky place.

"I delivered packages to rich people. I seen Edsel Ford once—he came in and bought a trench coat. He used to call in for shirts or ties. If you bought a tie there, you wouldn't see yourself coming and going. The ties were about three dollars."

On weekends Harry sold the *Detroit Free Press.*

"I hustled the Sunday morning paper by the Hoffman Hotel on Woodward Avenue. I'd get three hundred papers and I made a cent and a half on each one.

"With the five dollars I made at Capper and Capper, I was able to buy two meal tickets at a restaurant, the Busy Bee on Woodward. And we lived in that neighborhood, that was the rooming house district."

Harry was describing the same downtown Detroit neighborhood where Ruth Ellis lived, the streets and many of the buildings now familiar to me.

"One roomin' house had twelve rooms, another had three rooms. Another one just had an oversized clothes closet with a single bed in it. It didn't have any light in it and so we used to light a candle at night. But we got that room cheap. It was two dollars and fifty cents. And the bed we had was so narrow that my brother Bill never got so much hugging in his life. I had to hold him in my arms so he wouldn't fall."

Mr. Boeff's voice cracks.

"You were only kids," I say.

"Yeah. If the police had known, why, they would have put us in a detention home or sent us to Chicago."

He looks down at his lap.

"Were those hard times?" I ask.

He looks up and he's fighting tears.

"They were . . . when I think back . . ." He can't finish the sentence.

"You were having to take care of your little brother," I say.

"Yeah. We were eating our meals in a restaurant on a meal ticket. We were eating a lotta soup. And Bill was always punching my card. At the end of the month, if he runs out of his card, I'd tell him to punch mine, which he did. We got along, though. We didn't get in any trouble."

"There must have been some people watching out for you. At least they didn't turn you in, two kids alone."

"It was a tough neighborhood, you know. Drunken people and that. We'd get afraid sometimes of the class of people that was there, so we'd look for another room. All those land-ladies that we had and none of them ever invited us to a meal."

Mr. Boeff is sad and not angry. He wasn't abandoned, he made a bad choice.

"I don't know how we survived," he says.

"You know, Mr. Boeff, I'm amazed that your dad let you stay behind in Detroit. It's unimaginable to me that a father would leave two kids like that."

"Well, he had confidence in me. My dad said, 'Harry's a good boy. He knows what he's doing.' The last words he said to me, in German, were 'If anything happens, don't go to bed crying or lonesome. Send me a wire.' And I'd write to him almost every day and tell him how we were doing. I'd tell my dad in letters, from hour to hour, what we did. I said we were getting along good."

Finally, one of Harry's older brothers convinced him to come back to Rochester. He and Bill got jobs right away and soon Harry was making good money at a local shoe factory.

"Sixty dollars a week! I told my brother Bill, 'You're gonna have a brother who's a millionaire!' Every week I'd go to the bank on State Street, a block from where I worked, and I put my whole paycheck in there. I said, 'I'm gonna have a thousand dollars, and when I do, you won't be able to touch me,' and in no time, I had a thousand dollars in that bank."

Then Harry Boeff discovered parties and girls.

"In them days, everybody had a piana. You had a phonograph or a piana. What we would do, the girls would get together, six of them, and they'd know some fellas and there would be six boys and six girls and we'd go to this girl's house and play the piana, and we'd all sing, and the mother and father, they would be there, and the mother would make doughnuts and we'd have apple cider and play games. Every Saturday night there was a place to go for a party. At the first party I went to, I got Detroit out of my mind. I didn't even think of girls in Detroit, and here, these girls were all nice, down-to-earth girls. I just fell in love with all of them."

These memories are so clear to him. He is seeing those

girls in his mind and he radiates joy. It was 1920 when he decided to get married.

"Mr. Boeff, will you tell me that story?"

"Well, you just wouldn't believe it," he says. "I'm gonna tell you right from the beginning, just as it is. I always call her Mrs. Boeff, but I'm gonna call her Florence for you."

Mr. Boeff includes me in his storytelling. He isn't just remembering, he's talking to me. For every question I have, there's a story and he says, "Oh, you're gonna love this," or "This is a great one," as if he's been waiting for me to come here and ask him about his life. He's not self-centered; he is amazed at the events of his own life and at his own good memory, too. "See, I can remember pretty good," he'll say. His storytelling doesn't seem like a performance, but a generosity.

Maybe I'm just a better listener now than I was a year ago, not so worried about asking the "right" questions, not looking for the meaning of life, not looking for keys to my own future happiness. I'm just listening, finally, not analyzing or judging. It's a good feeling for me and for him, too, I think.

Mr. Boeff seems genuinely happy to have the chance to talk about Florence, to whom he was married seventy-six and a half years.

They had "kept company" for three years before they married. He's "kinda vague" on where they met. It might have been at one of those parties the year after he got back from Detroit, in about 1918.

Right around that time, the shoe factories in Rochester went on strike, nobody was working, and so Harry went fishing every day with some buddies. After a while, the other guys all got jobs with the railroad, but Harry wasn't big enough to do that kind of work, so he waited out the strike and eventually went back to the shoe factories. But while he was waiting, he got lonely for his fishing friends during the day and he could only see his girlfriend on certain nights.

"When you went out with a girl, you only went out on Tuesdays, Thursdays, and Saturdays. Them was date nights. If you took a girl out on any other night, like on Wednesday, people would say 'He's cheating' or 'She's cheating' because it wasn't date night.

"I got so lonely that I said, 'I'll go crazy if I don't get married,' so I went over to her house that night and I told her the story. I said, 'I'm down in the dumps and I want to get married.' And she said, 'When?' and I said, 'Tomorrow.' She said, 'We can't get married tomorrow, we gotta get ready.' And I said, 'Okay.'"

Three weeks later they got married and moved in with her grandparents. Harry Boeff made a family for himself so he would never feel the loneliness of those dark rooming houses in Detroit.

Harry and Florence moved onto Belmont Street in 1926, had a son, and stayed. Harry worked in the shoe factory, scrupulously saving money.

"I never bought stocks; that would be like gambling. The only thing I did, when I got ahold of my first ten thousand dollars, I bought a bank certificate. That's what I made my money on, outside of working with these hands. I had the house paid up in seven and a half years because I intended to stay here for the rest of my life."

"You mean from the beginning you knew?" I ask.

"I knew we would stay here. I liked it from the beginning. It had a big yard, we always had a garden. This has been our castle."

I've never known this feeling as an adult, that I would be in one place for the rest of my life. Somehow I think I should. Twice, my husband and I have bought houses and both times the feeling flitted across my mind like the shadow of a bird, but it never stayed to sing. Maybe I've traveled too much, maybe I inherited a restless gene. I suppose it would be different if I had children. Maybe it's part of why I don't.

Harry Boeff's certainty intrigues me, too. At twenty-one he wanted to get married and stay in one place for the rest of his life. On my twenty-first birthday I woke up in a sleeping bag, having camped in an open field on the outskirts of Marrakesh in Morocco. I was only certain that I wanted more adventure.

Mr. Boeff never traveled around the world or even drove a car. He was happy to let Florence do the driving. He had a good job, a house with a big yard and a sleeping porch. Sometimes he and Mrs. Boeff would sleep out there, he says, "look at the moon and talk ourselves to sleep." He loved his wife and his baby boy. He wasn't lonely. He wasn't searching. Harry Boeff had everything he wanted by the time he was thirty.

On Belmont Street he knew everyone. He lent out tools, he gave advice. Once, when a neighbor lady fainted, her husband came running for Harry. He went to help and told their kids, "Stand back and start praying," but the lady died in his arms.

The only person who's lived on the street longer than Harry is a woman named Catherine, who's eighty-eight now.

She was in high school when he moved here. Her husband died when she was in her forties, leaving her with three girls. Harry looked in on them every day. He can see her house across the street.

Today he can recite the history of every house up and down the block: who moved in, who moved out. He is especially close to the Moshers next door. Barbara does his grocery shopping and every morning she checks his porch to see that he has brought his paper in. If it's still there at nine o'clock, she knocks on his door. Pandora, her sheepdog, spends hours with Mr. Boeff. She pads around with him in the backyard when the weather is nice, checking on the raspberries.

Mr. Boeff retired from the shoe factory on the very day he was eligible. He says he kissed the front door good-bye and never went back.

"I wanted to forget it. I realized, 'They got the best years of my life and now that I'm free as a bird, I'm gonna fly from tree to tree and enjoy myself with my baby'—that was Florence—and we did."

They decided to travel, but first he had to put things in order. The first year he repainted the house. The second year he got dentures. ("Gee, I'm really telling you everything, aren't I?") They decided on Fort Lauderdale and went back to the same tourist home every year.

"We enjoyed every bit of our retirement," he says, "until towards the end, when she wasn't too well."

They stopped traveling in the 1980s because arthritis had weakened Florence's legs and then, in 1990, she had a stroke. Mr. Boeff cared for her at home but there were times when she couldn't eat. "I told her to stick it out, which she did," he says. "I got her so she was eatin' pretty good." He made vanilla pudding, grilled cheese sandwiches, hot dogs, "Whatever she wanted," he says. Mrs. Mosher says she used to hear Mr. Boeff sing to Florence every morning in the kitchen from her house next door. He did his best. She lived to age 96.

"I took her to the hospital on Saturday and on Sunday she died. It was so sudden it was kinda hard to pull yourself together. When she was laid out, I only went once. I figured that was all I could stand. And then we had a big snowstorm and they couldn't take her to the cemetery. That was all right with me. I couldn't stand to get in that car and go block after block. I just couldn't take care of it. I couldn't even do any of the things that had to be done. I just handed my checkbook to my son, Harry, and said, 'You take care of everything,' and he did."

Night has been the hardest time for Mr. Boeff. He and Florence had separate bedrooms, across the hall from each other.

"She used to call me Buffy, or sometimes Harry, or sometimes Daddy, and believe it or not, this one night, just as plain as she was there, I heard her say, 'Buffy!' And I hollered, 'What?' And that was all there was to it. So now I keep the door to her bedroom closed and I just pass it going to the bathroom or going to bed. I just let it go at that."

He looks down shyly.

"The first few months were terrible, you know?" he says. "You sit at the table and you're all alone. I have a friend named Gordon, his wife died just after Mrs. Boeff, and he talks as if he's gonna commit suicide, you know? And I tell him, 'Lookit. Show the world that you're a man, see? Be strong. And ask for help.'"

He points to the sky.

"You'll be all right."

MR. BOEFF AND I talked for two long days. There was nothing he wouldn't tell and, it seemed, nothing he couldn't remember. He can tell entire life stories about people he once knew, complete with quotations, and never lose his way or digress. He showed me his wedding picture, the contents of his freezer, the place where he sat by the kitchen window with Florence. He gave me cold apples and glasses of water and told me about his favorite TV shows. (He watches what he calls "the judges" every day, three courtroom programs in a row.) He remembers kids swimming in the Erie Canal. He remembers his aunt reading aloud the accounts of the *Titanic* disaster. He recalls selling newspapers on the street in Detroit in 1914 when the headline said WAR. He told me jokes he'd heard in vaudeville shows. He remembers the name of the piano roll tune his upstairs neighbor played day after day ("That Old Gang of Mine"). He remembers listening to radio station KDKA from Pittsburgh on his crystal set, and he remembers the day the founder of Eastman Kodak, George Eastman, killed himself in his mansion not far from here. (He and Florence drove by the house shortly afterward. "I always wonder if he was laying on the floor when we drove by," he says.)

He remembers huge parades in downtown Rochester to

celebrate President Roosevelt's National Recovery Act, and he told me about air-raid drills on Belmont Street during the war. He remembers the neighbors coming over to eat doughnuts and watch the fights when he was the first one on the block with a television.

But finally I had to leave. A big snowstorm was coming and so was Thanksgiving. I didn't feel the bittersweet sadness I had so many times before when I said good-bye to other centenarians. I felt certain that I would see Mr. Boeff again. He'd only just turned one hundred, his health was excellent, and if he could make it through the winter, when it was so hard to get out, he'd be fine, I thought.

We stood at the window, looking out toward his frozen backyard and the garage where Mrs. Boeff's car still waits. He invited me to come back in the summer. He showed me where the lawn chairs would be set up. We could sit and talk and watch the bird feeder and admire the raspberry patch. "You know, I started out with three bushes forty-two years ago," he says, "and that's the result."

"Who named those raspberries Boeff Beauties?" I ask.

"Well, they belong to Boeff, so I named them Boeff Beauties."

"How's the taste?"

"Outta this world. I've gotten as high as four hundred pints in a year."

"What happens to all those raspberries?"

"I give them to all my friends," he says, "and I have no enemies."

"You know," he says, "if you don't have any enemies, you don't have anything to fear."

AFTERWORD

WHEN YOU'RE one hundred years old, your life expectancy
is only a couple of years, at most. I knew that when I started
interviewing centenarians, but it didn't prepare me. Victoria
Williams, in Washington, D.C., died first, then Ella Miller, in
Virginia, and Mona Breckner, in Minnesota. Ruth Ellis died at
home in Detroit six months after I met her. Margaret Rawson
passed peacefully at home among friends, in Frederick, Maryland, as did Marion Cowen, in his apartment overlooking the
Pacific Ocean in San Francisco.

R. L. Stamper, at the ranch in Oklahoma, had just nine
months with his bride, Josephine. She went to his funeral in
the morning and then went back home to her own family in
Shreveport that afternoon. Gilbert Hill lost Sadie last summer, one month after their eighty-first wedding anniversary,
and he is struggling to adjust at home in central Florida. He
told a newspaper reporter, "She was the biggest half of me."
Harry Shapiro is alone now, too, in New York City, and he's
finding it harder to paint, he says, because "something wells
up inside me."

Recently I called Mr. Boeff at home in Rochester, as I do
now and then. He had surgery this past winter, and though
he hated being away from home, he was pleased that nurses

came from all over the hospital to get a look at a hundred-year-old man. On the phone he sang me old songs and told me jokes and said he's got raspberries waiting in the freezer for me. I visited him last summer and accepted his offer to stay overnight in his spare room. He cooked me a fine dinner of chicken wings and potatoes and set out some instant oatmeal for me in the morning.

I've spent more time with Anna Wilmot, too, at her home on the lake in western Massachusetts. Someone stole her oars last summer and the news was picked up by the Associated Press, so she's a local celebrity now. Winter is tough on her. The arthritis in her knees is bad. But she's promised to take me out in the boat this summer when I come for her 104th birthday party.

Professor Goldstein is still tutoring at Baruch College at age 103. A colleague of his told me she ran into him at the grocery store not long ago. I saw Helen Boardman just before Christmas. She spoke at the Governor's Conference on Aging in Chicago for 25 minutes without notes and received a standing ovation. Louisiana Hines is thriving, too, still in her home on the west side of Detroit.

New centenarians are coming into my life now. I've interviewed a lady whom demographers call a "supercentenarian"— over 110 years old. Her name is Verona Calhoun Johnston, and she was born in 1890. Her vision is poor, but she is alert and spunky. And this morning as I sat at my computer, a photo popped up on the screen of "the world's oldest man," Yukichi Chuganji of Japan, born March 23, 1889. He is sitting regally on a futon, a younger woman—his daughter? wife? a reporter?—beside him. His face is smooth and radiant; he has long earlobes and his head is crowned by a fog of wispy hair.

And, of course, I'm an avid reader of the obituaries now, looking for centenarians and aching a little bit when I read about one I would like to have met, like Harley Utz of Green-ville, Ohio, who died at 103 and was married eighty-three years, and Frieda Mae Hardin, who joined the U.S. Navy in 1914. I never got to meet Maude Rutherford, either, who had been a dancer at the Cotton Club in Harlem, and claimed to have introduced the Charleston to Broadway. I also missed Sister Martha Pellow, age 111, the nation's oldest nun, and a 107-year-old fellow from Washington, D.C., named Preston Williams, a former conductor on horse-drawn streetcars who left his body to the Georgetown University Medical Center because "somebody might want to find out why I never died."

I'm well aware that for every sharp, funny, charismatic centenarian I've met, there are three or four who are ailing, depressed, and alone. Probably not much fuss is made over them. I don't know how we change that, but Ruth Ellis's admonition to "remember the seniors," and her simple re-minder to say hello to someone who is sitting alone, is the starting place.

My father's father, Nikola Elezovich, died when I was fourteen, and I didn't know him very well. I thought he was mysterious and distant. He came to the United States as a teenager from the island of Šolta, off the coast of Croatia. He never spoke much English, but my father reminds me often about how wise and caring my grandfather was. He was fond of saying, "It doesn't cost anything to say hello," but I had to go out in the world and hear this from a stranger before it sank in.

My grandmother Riketa will celebrate her one hundredth birthday this summer. We're planning a big party for her, of course, but we're all fearful that she might not make it. She's been frail and withdrawn lately. This past January she met my sister's new baby, Isaac, for the first time. As we walked slowly from her bedroom to the living room, her ankles badly swollen, she took my arm and held her other hand up to the wall to steady herself. I noticed her arm had gotten so thin that her watch was pushed up to nearly her elbow. When she saw her new great-grandson, though, a light came over her face that I had not seen in a long time.

She's always been a demanding person, blunt and opinionated, but she never forgets our birthdays, and seems truly grateful for how far she has come in her life. Like my grandfather, she was born on a rocky island in the Adriatic Sea, where she carried water from the well on her head and baked bread in the community oven. She's always been full of well-meaning advice, too, but hers comes out slightly mangled because, as she says, "I forgot my own language and I never learned English." When I left for college, she told me, "Take care of your brain. You might need it someday."

I feel nervous about my grandmother's passing. I can't imagine my life when the people I love most are on the other side of the river. At four in the morning I wake up and worry that I will be the last one left, that living a long life will not be a gift but a nightmare. But most of the time I am hopeful that things will turn out well and I know I have choices. My family and my centenarians have shown me what's most important in life and I know the rest is up to me.

NEENAH ELLIS

March 2002

Takoma Park, Maryland

ACKNOWLEDGMENTS

MEMORY IS elusive and unreliable. I recorded my interviews with all the centenarians, but I couldn't capture every moment on tape and sometimes it was best to just sit and listen. I was able to check some facts and dates, but mostly I have related their stories as they remembered them.

I didn't verify their ages, either, and there are some whose age I have reason to doubt, but what's a few dozen months when you've lived that long, anyway?

I have many people to thank for their help. First is Stephanie Jenz. She suggested the radio project and helped me find centenarians to interview. Her judgment is unerring, and she has a caring way with the centenarians and their families and friends.

In addition to those mentioned in the text, I'd like to thank Edward Merritt, Helen Catchings, Bill Lyons, Freddie and Lilli Wilmot, Zane Berzins, Susan Stamberg, Margaret and Tom West, Joan Uchitelle, Kenneth Hill, Irene Thornton, Polly Pettit, Tonja Stamper, Reverend Richard Ziglar, Don and Janet Boardman, Paul Bridges, Mike Maxwell, Dave Knego, Tish Valva, Margaret Howze, Edie and Randy Crowder, and Marion Brodarick for sending me newspaper clippings and introducing me to centenarians.

The radio series "One Hundred Years of Stories" was

funded by the Corporation for Public Broadcasting. Thank you, Rick Madden and Jeff Ramirez.

Thanks to the staff at NPR's *Morning Edition*, especially Neva Grant, Ellen McDonnell, Jeffrey Katz, and Andrea Seabrook. And thank you, Flawn Williams, audio engineer extraordinaire and good friend.

Thank you, Katie Davis, Freya Manfred, and Joan Ringelheim for reading drafts with so much care. Jonathon Lazear and Steve Ross were relentlessly encouraging and Annik LaFarge came along as my energy waned and lifted me up like a kite in a fresh breeze.

And to my sweetest buddy and husband, Noah Adams, thank you for everything, forever.

About the Author

NEENAH ELLIS, formerly a staff producer for NPR's *All Things Considered,* is a freelance reporter and producer who has worked for the Discovery Channel, NPR, the U.S. Holocaust Memorial Museum, and the National Park Service. She lives with her husband, Noah Adams, in Takoma Park, Maryland.